For the Love of Music

Also by John Mauceri

Maestros and Their Music:
The Art and Alchemy of Conducting

For the Love of Music

A Conductor's Guide to the Art of Listening

JOHN MAUCERI

WEIDENFELD & NICOLSON

First published in the United States in 2019 by Alfred A. Knopf,
a division of Penguin Random House LLC

First published in Great Britain in 2020 by Weidenfeld & Nicolson
an imprint of The Orion Publishing Group Ltd
Carmelite House, 50 Victoria Embankment
London EC4Y 0DZ

An Hachette UK Company

1 3 5 7 9 10 8 6 4 2

Illustration Credits Page 2: John Mauceri; page 19: New York Public
Library, Manuscripts and Archives Division; page 33: XXX; page 51:
Hulton Archive / Getty; page 71: Getty Research Institute,
Los Angeles (980039); page 93: Gordon Parks / Getty; page 111: Starus
/ used under Creative Commons Attribution Share Alike 3.0 Unported
license (image altered); page 145: Library of Congress, Music Division,
Dayton C. Miller Collection; page 179: Johann Anton Völlner

A CIP catalogue record for this book is
available from the British Library.

ISBN (Hardback) 978 1 4746 1829 8
ISBN (eBook) 978 1 4746 1831 1

Printed and bound in Great Britain by Clays Ltd, Elcograf S.p.A

MIX
Paper from
responsible sources
FSC® C104740
www.fsc.org

www.weidenfeldandnicolson.co.uk
www.orionbooks.co.uk

For Aunt Rose, Aunt Jennie, and my brother Bob . . .

. . . and Lenny, of course

You may be sitting in a room reading this book. Imagine one note struck upon the piano. Immediately that one note is enough to change the atmosphere of the room—proving that the sound element in music is a powerful and mysterious agent, which it would be foolish to deride or belittle.

—AARON COPLAND, *What to Listen for in Music*

Contents

Introduction   3

CHAPTER 1   Why Music?   9

CHAPTER 2   The Heart of the Matter   19

CHAPTER 3   Harnessing (Human) Nature   33

CHAPTER 4   Time: Real and Imaginary   49

CHAPTER 5   Invisible Structures   69

CHAPTER 6   Pay Attention!   91

CHAPTER 7   The First Time:

Weaving the Web of Continuity   109

CHAPTER 8   The Concert Experience   143

CHAPTER 9   Your Playlist, Your Life   177

Acknowledgments   197

Index   201

For the Love of Music

Carnegie Hall. The audience arrives. January 2017

Introduction

I SAT ANONYMOUSLY in the top balcony of Carnegie Hall surrounded by 2,800 strangers who had come together on a Sunday afternoon to sit in the dark and listen to the music of Mozart and Bruckner. The sounds of the city—automobile and truck horns, the rumble of the subway beneath our feet, the occasional siren—were erased by the buzz of conversation in the hall, building in a gentle crescendo as a sold-out house settled in. Winter coats stuffed under our seats, a perfunctory hello extended to our temporary neighbors, we perused our programs and waited for the lights to dim. Members of the Staatskapelle Berlin, an orchestra that traces its history back to 1570, entered the stage and took their places around a grand piano with its lid removed.

Our corporeality soon melted away as the stage glowed, focusing our attention on the musicians below us. Daniel Barenboim, serving as both conductor and pianist, entered to great applause. He sat down—his back to us—and, with a gesture from his right hand, there was music, Mozart's Piano Concerto no. 23.

A sweet and pulsing A-major chord rose in the air, gentle and elegant. It was no longer a matter of where we were or what year it was—the music was timeless, eternal, and utterly beautiful. When the second movement began, with Barenboim's solo statement of a sad and wistful melody of intimate musings, a different pulse—like a barcarolle's lulling—accompanied the give-and-take between the piano and the orchestra in a wordless aria: a meditation, really, one that seemed to embrace regrets, consolation, and gentle laughter. And without a moment's hesitation, the entire ensemble leaped into the final movement: thousands of cascading notes, scampering woodwinds, and joyous melodies brought all of us into a celebration of life itself—sunshine and clouds all together in an ideal environment of civility and musicianship.

And we were only halfway through the concert.

Returning to my seat after the break, I could not help wondering at what I was now seeing on the stage. Instead of a grand piano and a small orchestra, a hundred musicians filled the entire floor space. Where there had been two French horns for Mozart, there were now eight! Woodwinds and strings had been multiplied, and my eyes began to prepare me for what my ears would soon hear—an entirely different universe of sound.

Bruckner, like Mozart, was an Austrian Catholic. Unlike Mozart, he was a devout believer whose goal was to express the greatness of God in every note he composed. As a boy from a little town, he never got over the experience of being a choirboy at a nearby monastery with its magnificent baroque architecture and grand pipe organ, which he was occasionally allowed to play. The sound of his adolescence at St. Florian's Augustinian monastery became the guiding acoustical and structural template for the grand and enormous symphonies of his adulthood.

The Ninth is Bruckner's last symphony, left incomplete at

the time of his death in 1896, and composed during a period in which he was aware of his terminal illness. When we experience its three movements we stand before the gate separating life from death.

Beginning with an almost inaudible trembling in the strings, we are in the key of D minor, and not by chance. This is the key of Beethoven's last symphony, also numbered nine, and as we do with Beethoven, we enter its realm in devout quiet. It is a quiet that pulls all of us in. From its mysterious opening bars we hear a low, heroic melody on the eight horns, and within two minutes there is an earth-shattering statement by the orchestra that resets our senses to this new and immense cosmos of possibilities.

Themes of intense longing, beauty, and weariness intermingled as Bruckner—through Barenboim and his Berlin orchestra—took us on an exploration of towering majesty and human frailty in a play of dynamics that includes moments of total silence before each mighty ascent. Writers have described Bruckner's symphonies as Gothic cathedrals of sound, and in many ways they are—but they are late-nineteenth-century imaginary cathedrals, as epitomized by the cathedral in Cologne that was begun in 1248 but not completed until 1880. Where there had once been stonecutters in the Dark Ages, there were now nineteenth-century engineers supervising workers who were pouring concrete into molds. That Bruckner's Ninth was left incomplete makes it a perfect metaphor for the very thing it emulated—the unfinished work of humans to serve and celebrate God.

This concert was a celebration of many things, of course. Ostensibly it marked the sixtieth anniversary of Barenboim's Carnegie Hall debut in 1957 and was the culmination of a week of concerts in which he shared his mastery as a pianist and a conductor, performing works by two of the most significant composers of classical music, and he did it all with a technical skill that few musicians could ever duplicate.

Sitting there that afternoon, I also felt a communion—not just with those who were in the audience, but also with the thousands of people who have sat in that very same place ever since the opening concerts in 1891, when Tchaikovsky journeyed from Moscow to conduct his music there. Every person who sits in that seat is celebrating continuity.

As we shall see, classical music celebrates community, nature, humanity's aspirations, triumphs, and foibles, and our desire to apply form to chaos. It reaches back to the very beginnings of what it means to be human.

It's a mystery, after all—music. Why do we compose it, perform it, and why does everyone listen to it? All living things create the conditions for survival. To that, humans can uniquely add music—which fundamentally is the organization of vibrations in the air that brings joy and communality. We move our bodies to it; we sing it; we celebrate spirituality with it; we commemorate and memorialize with it; we march to war with it; we play it whenever we wish to create an environment of importance—weddings, funerals, high-school graduations. And sometimes we buy a ticket to sit in the dark in the top balcony of Carnegie Hall to hear Mozart and Bruckner on a Sunday afternoon.

When the concert was over, we exited onto Fifty-Seventh Street and Seventh Avenue. It was already dark, and the temperature was dropping rapidly. The temporary community that had come together and experienced something collectively—now only a memory and a printed program—went their separate ways. Messages from 1786 and 1896 had been sent to us via an orchestra of Berliners and its music director—a citizen of Argentina, Israel, Palestine, and Spain—in New York City in 2017. A sense of satisfaction within all of us was now being dispersed into a city of eight million people. Each of us carried something inside us that was, for lack of a more poetic word, good.

In the succeeding pages, while exploring the art of listening, I hope to tell you why classical music is the epitome of Western art and human expression, and to show you how a local phenomenon that developed in Europe in the early 1700s has become a global one—one that erases any sense of West and East. Viewed from above, the earth has no dotted lines that separate countries and cultures.

Barenboim would understand, of course. He is also the cofounder (with the late Palestinian-American cultural critic Edward Said) of the West-Eastern Divan Orchestra, a youth orchestra of Israelis, Palestinians, Arabs, and Iranians—primarily Jews and Muslims—that plays music composed by dead white European men, most of whom were Christians. One young member of the group referred to it as "a human laboratory." Like Doctors Without Borders, the music they play carries something universal within it that has the power to heal.

Classical music offers us so much—and so much to relish. It can be enjoyed at a given moment and over a lifetime. It can change its shape and form as we change ours. My goal here is to help you enjoy it more. With classical music, there is always more.

CHAPTER I

Why Music?

Pythagoras (c. 570–c. 495 BC), seen as the father of music for
over a thousand years, is here represented in an image by Leonardo
da Vinci's contemporary and friend Franchino Gaffurio, in his
Theorica musicae, published in 1492. Notice how the notes being
played are determined by mathematical relationships.

MUSIC IS A WORK OF HUMAN IMAGINATION. It is also invisible. Experienced through time, it must be allowed to *take its time* in order for it to be understood. It is protean, since its outlines can be recognized and repeated but it can never be exactly the same twice. That's because no two performances of the same piece of music—given the myriad choices made at every moment in performing it—can be exactly the same; and you, the listener, are never the same, even when you replay a favorite recording. You are in "a different place," as the common phrase goes, and that place has to do with time and experience.

We surely will never get to the bottom of why we make music, even if we look for similarities in other life forms, like the "songs" of whales and birds. But it is worth considering that music is a uniquely human creation, and its function does not make any sense in terms of Darwinian hypotheses of species survival and natural selection. We cannot derive food from it. We cannot protect our family with it. Perhaps its magnificence can be traced to its persistence in spite of its seemingly inexplicable uselessness.

Since we are considering a certain kind of music, we should define our terms.

What Is Western Music?

The term "Western music" refers to music that was first described by the foundational fathers of what has been called

"Western culture"—the Greeks. This title should probably be banished, since it implies a fundamental boundary that was invented by scholars to differentiate Europe from Asia and Africa. "West of what?" might be a question we should ask. Indeed, many Greek texts would otherwise have been lost were it not for Arab translations and commentaries emanating from the medieval Islamic world. That said, I will continue to occasionally use the phrase to mean music that has developed from the Greek descriptions of a specific kind of music.

The Greeks organized music by modes (we call them scales today), and those modes were called by the names of their various indigenous tribes, including Dorians, Aeolians, and Lydians. Music in the Phrygian mode, for example, was believed to represent the characteristics of the Phrygian people who lived in the mountainous region in what is now western Turkey. They also believed that if you played music in the Phrygian mode, it would make you behave as if you actually were a Phrygian—i.e., unruly and passionate. Music controlled behavior through description and by creating an environment that transcended and transformed the tangible world around us.

For the Greeks, music also governed the functioning of the cosmos—the physics of what we saw and felt, translated into what we heard. Indeed, they believed there is an ur-music we cannot perceive as humans, the exquisite cosmic music that Philo of Alexandria (20 BC–50 AD) said Moses heard when he received the tablets on Mount Sinai, and which St. Augustine believed was heard by us mortals only at the moment of our death. Our earthly music is a subset of the Music of the Spheres. This is the heart and soul of Western music and its language. Based on a concept of a home key (its mode or scale) and the perception that faster vibrations are literally higher (as in physically higher) than slower ones, the distance *between* notes in a melody signifies important emotional information that the populace intrinsically understands. This is the core of a descriptive language, simple in its basics and astonishingly varied in its application when creating new music.

The Romans carried the music of the Greeks throughout the world and found that the indigenous music of the peoples it subsumed into their empire could be enfolded into Greco-Roman music's basic language. As the centuries passed, Western music—acquisitive, adaptive, omnivorous—continued to develop and embrace a world of gestures and colors, always founded on the laws of nature (the physics of a vibrating string or the air passing through a hollow tube) and the observations of the ancient Greeks. Pythagoras showed how mathematics (proportions and ratios) and music are intertwined, and how the movements of the stars and planets, as well as the notes that emanated from their panpipes and lyres, all behaved according to the same principles.

An octave, for example, can be achieved by shortening a vibrating string to half its length. The same thing happens when you cut hollow reeds and blow across the top. A reed that is half as long as another will sound an octave higher than the longer one. Nature and the cosmos itself were all music. The movement of the stars, it was said, produces harmony. For the founders of Greco-Roman civilization, music was included in what became known as the *quadrivium* (arithmetic, geometry, music, and astronomy) and together with the *trivium* (grammar, logic, and rhetoric) comprised the seven liberal arts. Music also controlled the function of the human body. In other words, music was understood to describe and control just about everything inside and surrounding us. No wonder there are people who do not think of our species as

Homo sapiens, wise hominids, but rather *Homo narcissus.* It is always about us.

With these unprecedented concepts—that music is the engine that operates the entire universe, from the atomic level to the celestial; that music has the capacity to describe the characteristics of people and places; and that it can transform our behavior—the Greeks established what is known as Western music. To honor them we use their word for it—*mousiki.* It is the word for this miraculous invention in English, Swahili, Arabic, Uzbek, Ukrainian, Russian, Danish, German, Basque, Latin, and all the Romance languages.

Western music is the foundational language of Bach, Gregorian chant, Palestrina, Verdi, Gershwin, the waltz, rock and roll, and jazz.

What Do We Mean by the Term "Classical Music"?

Musicologists have a fairly narrow definition of what constitutes classical music, but the general public does not. The term itself was not used until the early nineteenth century. Technically all music that predates 500 AD is called ancient music. What followed is early music, the first music in history that we can attempt to replicate by performing it using notational systems we can decipher. Thus, early music is the music of the Middle Ages, the Renaissance, and the early baroque (up to about 1710).

When you consider that humans have inhabited the earth for some 200,000 years, we have a very small understanding of what our first music was, how it developed, and what it sounded like. There are no images on a cave wall for music and just a few artifacts of what we think are instruments. The further we probe back in time toward the year 500 the more controversy there is as to what the written symbols representing music actually meant, assuming there are any. For many centuries music was passed on through repetition and imitation, not from reading notes on a page. How it developed and morphed during that time is therefore impossible to determine.

With the exception of music from the Catholic Church, most of this early music had simply disappeared from performance and had to be revived, if at all possible, through scholarship—much of which happened in the twentieth century. What the public considers classical music—as shall we—begins in the first decades of the eighteenth century, what historians call the high baroque era. Historians will refer to the next period (the music of Haydn and Mozart) as classical, followed by the Romantic era (Beethoven and Schubert in the early 1800s and stretching into the last years of the nineteenth century), which is followed by the modern era (itself often broken into categories like impressionism, expressionism, experimental, and the current postmodern era, which includes minimalism).

Eras do not start and stop on specific days or in specific years. The concept of classical music, as generally understood by the public, means the music we hear played in chamber-music concerts, opera houses, and symphony orchestras, and includes not only the music played on modern instruments but also on replicas of instruments that fell into disuse and had to be re-created for music from earlier eras, i.e., early music and certain baroque works. However, the classical music canon—the central repertory—begins when modern instruments are used to play music, even though instruments continued to be developed during subsequent centuries. You are as likely to hear Handel's *Messiah* played by a contemporary baroque ensemble using replicas of old instruments as you are the London Symphony Orchestra playing on modern ones.

All art can be defined as the result of the human need to

organize the chaos of sensory input through mimicry and symbolism. For sight, it is painting. For the olfactory, it is cuisine and perfumes. For hearing, it is music. Art endeavors to stop time (portraiture, sculpture). It attempts to learn/teach lessons from the past (drama, literature). It creates supersaturated solutions of words and thoughts in poetry. It coalesces ideas in philosophy and politics. And it is pleasurable.

Psychologists are divided on whether all pleasure is the same thing. Brain scans show that pleasure, no matter what the source, registers similarly, but different kinds of pleasurable input activate additional neural systems. These relate to memory, reasoning, and a sense of self. In that way, scientists believe, not all pleasure is the same.

Unlike music, paintings pose the challenge of making something inert—an object hanging on a wall—into something interactive. Like music, art is perceived through time, but your eye will determine how it journeys into the frame, and your brain's pleasure centers will determine just how much real time you give to the work.

Attending a play will be pleasurable when you lose yourself in its nonreality (accepting an actor as being Julius Caesar) and the techniques of stagecraft—what Samuel Taylor Coleridge called in 1817 "the willing suspension of disbelief . . . or poetic faith." It is not just willingness, mind you—humans seem to crave illusion and enjoy "pretend." When a talking portrait of the long-dead wizard Albus Dumbledore says to a grown-up Harry Potter, "I am paint and memory," the words might be summing up the arts in general. However, paint does not stick to every surface, and so it is with the arts, and music specifically.

But if drama is pretend, music is metaphor.

One of the basic elements of classical music is that it acts as a descriptive and narrative language of vibrations, organized by scales and harmonies that are chosen to act as symbolic of how we humans experience the universe around us.

Classical music takes the legacy of music that has emerged over the centuries—the dances, the songs, and the sounds we hear—and manipulates them into something bigger and more meaningful. The elements of classical music are derived from two sources: the twelve notes that divide up the octave and supply the source of its melodies, and the pulses that inform the melodies and support them in a series of accented and unaccented beats, usually repeating in patterns of twos, threes, and fours. These are the meters and the rhythms. And from these two simple ingredients gigantic edifices of time can be constructed. Some classical compositions are intimate, involving one or two performers, and some are quite short, like a song by Schubert. What these works share with the mighty operas of Wagner and the enormous symphonies of Mahler is the application of genius to make something that feels inevitable and profound out of something so naively simple.

I firmly believe, and hope to explain, how classical music communicates, through distillation and form, a sense of proportion and order, all delivered through a series of metaphors for life experiences: emotional, spiritual, and reasonable. We musicians tell our stories through this extraordinary invisible medium. That makes it easier for you to relate to the story, because you, the listener, ultimately make it about yourself, and—this is the personal part—you get to finish the story. Delivering it to you, if you accept the gift, it becomes yours. It is not too much of a stretch, therefore, to say that the classical music you come to embrace ultimately becomes part of your autobiography.

CHAPTER 2

The Heart of the Matter

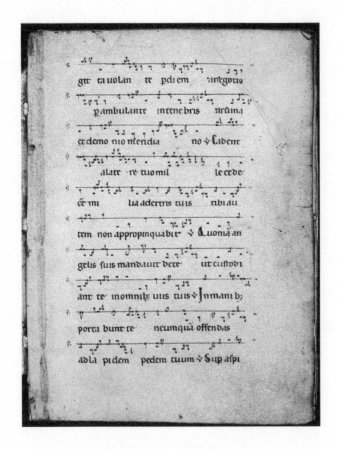

Notation before modern musical notation was fixed is represented
in this parchment example from a twelfth-century manuscript.
It took musicologists in the late 1800s and early 1900s to
translate centuries of Western musical notation into music
that could be read and understood.

CLASSICAL MUSIC—a subsection of "Western music," which is a subsection of world music—has another unique component: at its heart it is demarcated by a fairly short chronological period, something less than 250 years. It is not that there wasn't classical music before 1700, or that composers weren't—and aren't—writing it after 1940. What is odd is what the public has come to embrace, and therefore what it has rejected. During the sixty years I have been attending and performing classical music, the standard repertory— the works you are most likely to hear in a concert—has hardly changed.

These works constitute the core of the vast majority of concerts and operas given throughout the world, sometimes referred to as the "canon," a word that appropriately comes from the Greek, meaning "rule." Thus, in religious studies, the canon is a collection of sacred texts that are deemed to be genuine. In other words, this is the music you are going to hear whenever or wherever you attend a classical music performance.

Only one composer, the proto-cinematic Gustav Mahler (1860–1911), went from a marginal figure in the first half of the twentieth century to become part of the central symphonic repertory in the 1960s. Similarly, Sergei Rachmaninoff (1873–1943), who was always being performed but was often dismissed as a lightweight composer of old-fashioned Russian Romanticism, is now accepted as a serious composer. To this, we can add one opera—Puccini's last (and unfinished) *Turandot*, premiered in 1926, which is now a staple in operatic repertory due to the confluence of (1) the emergence of a great dramatic soprano, Birgit Nilsson, to sing the difficult title role with (2) the development of high-fidelity stereo recording techniques that made it a sonic blockbuster in the 1960s. While *Turandot* had never completely disappeared after its world premiere, it was hardly the central work it has become, additionally aided by the phenomenal popularity of its act-three aria "Nessun Dorma!" after Luciano Pavarotti sang it at the 1990 World Cup on global television. No other operas can claim this new centrality, even though the magnificent operas of Berg, Britten, and Janáček have appeared with a certain regularity in major opera houses during the past half century. Indeed, new operas are being produced with regularity and with success. It remains to be seen if any of the most recent works will have the staying power of the central works—and, indeed, if "staying power" is even a viable criterion.

There are, needless to say, passionate supporters of classical music on either "side" of what one might call its Golden Age, but all the proselytizing and arguments cannot seem to widen the embrace of the canonic works, also known as the standard repertory. This is not true of visual art, literature, dance, or theater, including musical theater. A new musical play like Lin-Manuel Miranda's 2015 *Hamilton* can attract hundreds of thousands of people who will pay enormous sums of money to see it and simultaneously can garner such prestigious awards as the Pulitzer Prize.

Visual art, for example, is collected, bought, sold, hung on the walls of our greatest museums, and owned by the wealthiest people in the world. It covers an enormous period of time, from the very first artifacts of humanity to brand-new works. The public has demonstrated an acceptance of, fascination with, and love for the colors, textures, and forms found in ancient and modern art, and from every culture and time period. During the twentieth century, for example, symbolism, realism, primitivism, cubism, impressionism, surrealism, and postmodernism—indeed, every "ism"—have enough popular support to justify major exhibitions in museums and galleries, along with a level of commercial and cultural value that encourages countries, foundations, and private-citizen groups to engage in lawsuits over their ownership.

Dance in the second half of the twentieth century was as vital as ever before, arguably even more so, with the fulfillment of the promise from choreographers like George Balanchine, Martha Graham, Alvin Ailey, Jerome Robbins, Merce Cunningham, Katherine Dunham, Agnes de Mille, and Paul Taylor—just to name Americans who have passed away. These people and dozens more from all over the world created enduring twentieth-century masterpieces that added new and exciting repertory to dance companies—some of which are devoted exclusively to their works. In the first quarter of the twenty-first century, living choreographers including Alexei Ratmansky, Twyla Tharp, Mark Morris, Annabelle Lopez Ochoa, Justin Peck, William Forsythe, and Christopher Wheeldon (and this is a very selective list) continue an unbroken line of dance that started in the Italian Renaissance and was developed in the French court of Louis XIV.

Classical music does not participate in this phenomenon of commercial and cultural value and ownership. Stubbornly remaining within a 250-year period, most of the music you will hear at concerts and opera houses is in the public domain, predating copyright laws. In other words, everyone on earth owns it, and it has no intrinsic monetary value.

What might also be pertinent here is that the determination of the chronological entry point to the core repertory was fixed around the same time the exit point was also determined—the interwar period (1918–39). The former was created by musicologists who had, in the first half of the twentieth century, developed the ways and means of restoring the lost music of the Renaissance and who insisted that it be played on replicas of ancient instruments. It was therefore not to be the province of existing classical music institutions of the early twentieth century, and required separate training and new institutions to perform it. In other words, you will not hear any of this music played by your local symphony orchestra or chamber music society. If you live near a university with an early music program, or in a city where such groups tour, you will have the joy of discovering this rich legacy of preclassical music.

The latter, the exit point, was created by the public, which rejected modernism and the experiments of the twentieth century's avant-garde with a near-universal consistency, even when those new works garnered temporary excitement, a good deal of newsprint, and the occasional scandal. The public, musicologists, and music critics, however, have found common ground and agreed on a finite window of time, a kind of aesthetic demilitarized zone, and the major compositions contained within its time frame, the uncontested classical works, have remained inflexible for more than a half century.

In our current environment music is available from so many periods and cultures that it may be surprising to imagine a time when a person had to commit to hearing music by going to a concert, attending High Mass, or learning to play an instrument in order to participate in performing chamber music with family and friends. Music had always been passed on through memory and repetition, and for centuries music created for special occasions was newly composed and quickly discarded. As already noted, it was not until the Middle Ages that the Catholic Church, in its desire to preserve its control and continuity, developed a notational system of visually representing its chants, sometimes called Gregorian chant, by which they could be performed anywhere the Gospel was preached, and without the presence of a composer to teach it. Outside of a church, it was unusual to hear music from earlier periods; and even if one desired to hear music of the past, there were no printing presses, and the only way to promulgate music was through hand-copied manuscripts.

When we think of classical music, we think of printed, engraved pages of notes floating on a series of five parallel lines and with many indications that tell a musician how the notes should sound—their speed, their length, and their general quality. That notational system developed very late in European history and over a long period of time. Even if you have been trained to read music, it's unlikely that you will be able to read the music from the Renaissance or before. It will look vaguely like music, but someone will have to tell you how to translate what is on the page, and even then you will not know about dynamics, rhythm, and tempo. You will not know how or whether to fill out the harmonies that are implied by the bass line, with nothing above it in some scores, or how to follow the meaning of numbers below the bass notes in others.

Although the basics of what we expect today in written music were in place by the end of the sixteenth century, notation continued to be refined into the twentieth. While an orchestral score of a Mahler symphony from around 1900 shares much the same basic information as a score by Beethoven from around 1800, the specificity in a Mahler score is incrementally far more complex, telling performers the precise speeds and tempo shifts, and also occasionally adding complete sentences from the composer in footnotes. (His

Symphony no. 5 begins with an asterisk before the very first note: "The upbeat triplet of this theme must be somewhat fleeting [quasi accelerant] in the style of a military fanfare.") Beethoven, on the other hand, will tell you a tempo at the start of a piece, indications of phrasing, and basic dynamics. After that, you are on your own.

Mind you, all musicians still have to interpret whatever notation they are studying, no matter how specific it is, and this allows for wide disparity among performances of the same piece, whether by Beethoven or Mahler. After all, how loud is "loud"? If Beethoven begins his Symphony no. 9 with the dynamic *pp* (*pianissimo*—i.e., very soft) and Tchaikovsky indicates that a bassoon solo in his Symphony no. 6 should be played *pppppp*, it's impossible to differentiate between them, because they come from two different works and from two different periods in the history of notation. No conductor could start a performance of Beethoven's Ninth thinking, "This should be quiet, but a lot louder than that transition in the first movement of Tchaikovsky's Sixth." What we do know is that both composers wanted these passages to be very quiet.

Our desire to hear music is hard-wired, and it took a newly invented field, musicology, to address the issue of resurrecting all the music found in dusty manuscripts in monasteries and to use rigid editorial principles to create modern editions of early music. That happened, as already noted, mostly in the first half of the twentieth century. The prolific French composer Josquin des Prez (d. 1521), for example, was considered to be the greatest composer of the age, but creating a comprehensible and comprehensive edition of his music did not begin until 1919. The work of teams of musicologists was not completed until 2016, with volume 29.

All of this leaves us with this sliver of time in which we

find the apex of human expression and world culture—the canonic works of classical music. It begins with the towering achievements of Johann Sebastian Bach, the divinely inspired architect, and George Frideric Handel, the great cosmopolitan entertainer. Our classical institutions begin their repertory with these two men, both Germans born in 1685, whose careers could not have been more different. Bach lived his entire life within Lutheran northern Germany, while Handel traveled to Catholic Italy, where he studied and composed church music for enormously wealthy cardinals, and then traveled to London, where he resided for many years, composing Italian opera and great English-language oratorios. Both men wrote chamber music, keyboard music, cantatas, and Masses. Unlike Bach, however, Handel was a hugely popular composer who attracted attention, adoration, and commercial riches in Rome and London. Bach was an employee of a small church in Leipzig and frequently complained about how little he was being paid for his services in providing a new cantata every week for the parishioners of the St. Thomas Church.

With Bach's Brandenburg Concertos (1721), his Cello Suites from 1723, his *St. Matthew Passion* (1727) and Mass in B Minor (1747), and Handel's *Water Music* of 1717, *Messiah* (1741), and *Royal Fireworks Music* (1749), we have entered the realm of universal greatness, recognized as such by the world and performed by our greatest musicians and ensembles, whether or not they are specialists in period instruments and historically informed performance practice.

From here it is a short journey to Haydn, who was born in 1732, when both Bach and Handel were still alive. It is Haydn who develops the genres of the string quartet (68 of them) and the symphony (106 of them) as we know them today. The young Mozart studied with Haydn and dedicated some string quartets to him. Indeed, they played chamber music together, with the older Haydn playing first violin and Mozart on the viola. And yes, the young Beethoven also studied with Haydn, who lived into the new century, dying in French-occupied Vienna in 1809. Franz Schubert, who also lived in Vienna at that time, was a torch bearer at Beethoven's funeral in 1827.

This astounding confluence of genius in these years solidified the Austro-German pride in being the ultimate creators of classical music. The line does not waver until the 1930s and the outbreak of World War II, when the racial policies of the Third Reich outlawed the music of some of the region's greatest contemporary composers: Kurt Weill, Arnold Schoenberg, Paul Hindemith, and Erich Wolfgang Korngold. They would all compose, inspire, and teach in the United States and die as American citizens. Only the aged Richard Strauss remained in Germany, where he lived in constant fear of his grandchildren's well-being, because his son had married a Jewish woman. With his death in 1949 in Switzerland, the story of German classical music that began with Bach and Handel came to an end.

Others will argue that last sentence, of course. The emergence of a post–World War II avant-garde and the musical theories of German musicologists and commentators dominated the discourse for much of the twentieth century, but none of the musical works composed by them has entered the central repertory, and they show little signs of doing so. It should also be said that the composers who forged their new music did so proudly, cutting their link to the German classical music traditions. Any composer who was seen as continuing those traditions, like Hindemith, Korngold, and the later Schoenberg, was summarily dismissed from their modern movement.

When we look at the other cultures that brought us the central repertory of classical music, specifically Italy and France, the story ends much the same way. Italy's justifiable pride in its musical legacy is linked with the Roman Catholic Church, the Renaissance, and the invention, in 1598, of opera. After World War II, the Italian orchestras and opera companies banned the music of any composer associated with the Fascist regime, which ostensibly meant every composer whose music was being performed in the state-run theaters and concert halls in the period from 1922 until 1945. The repertory therefore went backward to Italy's immense musical legacy and then skipped over the recent unacceptable political history of Mussolini to the new musical modernism of Luigi Nono and a school of like-minded contemporaries who broke with the Italian traditions of songful operas and symphonic works.

The French, whose language and culture became the international language of diplomacy, can see their culture as a worldwide phenomenon, tracing its musical heritage to the court of Louis XIV—who ruled France for an astounding seventy-two years (1643–1715)—and the development of ballet, and subsequently French grand opera, which made extensive use of dance. Later still, in the early twentieth century, Paris became the home of an international school of composers whose music is frequently called impressionism. Like West Germany and Italy, the French moved into a strictly modernist period after 1945, led by Pierre Boulez, and broke with its past and its continuity, purposefully and successfully.

Without creating lists of composers and their home countries, music is, as already noted, invisible, and it can sneak past borders without a passport. In the 250 years before the end of World War II, classical music emanating from the complex cultural history of Europe—and the dynamics of imperialism, invasions, wars, treaties, and trade—had already begun to be accepted into the cultures of much of the world.* This is hugely significant.

The European Jesuits, for example, carried classical music with them as they converted South America and Asia. Today, there are children in the jungles of Bolivia who play and know baroque music as a direct and unbroken legacy of the ideals brought to South America by priests who hoped to create a utopian society built from education, self-sustainability, faith, and music. If this music had not spoken to the Bolivians, it would not have persisted and would have disappeared with the Jesuits, who were expelled in 1767 and whose missions fell to ruins.

In North America, the Moravians from the Wachau region outside of Vienna brought European classical music to the New World. Unlike other Protestant sects that came to America and wanted nothing to do with music, the Moravians made music part of their service (a "necessity of life") and as a result not only carried the music of Haydn, Mozart, and the Bach family to their settlements in Bethlehem, Pennsylvania (1741), and Salem, North Carolina (1766), they also were the first to compose new classical music in America. This meant that the Founding Fathers of the United States who were interested in classical music, like Benjamin Franklin, journeyed to Moravian enclaves to hear Handel and Bach. It also meant that the Moravians played and taught this music to all, including their African servants as well as the Scots/Irish who passed

---

* It is also worth remembering that from 711 AD until 1492, most of what we call Spain and Portugal was under Islamic control. Given the life expectancy in that period, twenty-five generations of "Europeans" lived and died in a Muslim country singing the songs and dancing the dances that were brought into their Greco-Roman and Visigoth culture.

through Pennsylvania and North Carolina and moved into the mountains, where they adapted this music to create the roots music that is foundational to American folk music. The very same harmonic world of the Moravian church would contribute to gospel music and the blues. (At the same time, Moravian missionaries brought their beliefs and European music to the Caribbean islands of Saint Thomas, Saint John, and Saint Croix.)

Austro-German music had come to America before it was a country and became the language of both sacred and secular music that spread through the colonies and into the new century as its population moved westward. Simultaneously in Europe and Russia, Napoleon was emancipating Jews in every country he conquered, opening the ghettos and granting them rights as citizens who could own property and worship openly—and perform and compose music.

With developments in transportation in the early nineteenth century, travel—and therefore influence—led to an unprecedented internationalization of classical music. At international fairs, indigenous music from as far away as Java came to Paris in the late nineteenth century and was absorbed into the Western musical vocabulary of Debussy and Ravel, among others. In the first decades of the new century there were radio broadcasts and recordings of music. The world of music, which always was porous, was now wide open, and achieved the final glorious half-century that brought us Mahler, Sibelius, Debussy, Ravel, Falla, Puccini, Strauss, Rachmaninoff, Stravinsky, Prokofiev, and Schoenberg. In America, which had opened its borders to those fleeing the pogroms of Russia, three boys whose parents made the United States their new home would define American classical music—George Gershwin, Aaron Copland, and Leonard Bernstein.

How can we explain the world conquest of this musical language, a language that continually reinvents itself but never abandons its line back to the Greeks? Perhaps it is its continuity and its constant transformation that account for the dominance of the music and its ability to transcend indigenous musical expressions while simultaneously accepting their influences. It is neither a question of cultural appropriation nor one of simple cultural diffusion. No one forced the Japanese to love Beethoven's Ninth Symphony as a traditional way to welcome the new year. If the public did not want to hear it, it would not be programmed annually throughout the country. By its very nature, music is susceptible to the vicissitudes of taste. Japan, with a population of only 127 million, has nineteen official symphony orchestras. In the twenty-first century, China has been creating new symphony orchestras throughout its enormous country of 1.4 billion people. It is discovering the classical music that developed in Europe in the past two and a half centuries because people want to hear it and the government believes in its benefits to society. Classical music, though never without its challenges, is very much alive because people want to experience something precious and unique, something that is both simple and complex—a pleasurable riddle to be solved, perhaps.

At the heart of it, classical music is bound up in humanity's desire to tell its stories through symbols: languages made up of words, images, and sounds, and our need for communication and transference. Marcel Proust said it best in his *In Search of Lost Time*, when he wrote: "I wondered whether music might not be the unique example of what might have been—if the invention of language, the formation of words, the analysis of ideas had not intervened—the means of communication between souls."

CHAPTER 3

Harnessing (Human) Nature

King David Playing the Harp with Angels Dancing and Playing Music
by Peter Candid (1548–1628), Peter Sadeler, printmaker

IN A REAL SENSE, music harnesses nature, and by "nature" I mean both the natural world around us and the one that's inside us—also known as human nature. The beginnings of music are, of course, unknown to us, but they are not difficult to imagine. Humans are mimics, after all. We can utter myriad sounds from our vocal cords, mouths, and tongues. We walk and breathe in groups of twos—left/right, inhale/exhale; the speed of our heartbeats and our breaths vary with how we feel and what we are doing. All learning comes from curiosity, experimentation, and imitation, whether building a fire, singing, whistling, or discovering how a dried animal bone could make sounds by blowing into it. Hit a hollow log with a stick and you will want to hit it again.

The next time you attend a concert, consider for a moment the instruments themselves. Remove your thoughts from the music and the players and imagine the thousands of years of development that went into making a modern flute (at least thirty-five thousand years) or a harp (King David was a harpist).

Without a degree in archaeology, you can use your imagination to consider how a flute became a flute. Indeed, every instrument that is a tube and has air blown through it is fundamentally the same thing that once started as a bone, a piece of bamboo, the horns of an animal, or perhaps a conch shell. Our ancestors picked them up and inexplicably put them to their mouths and blew through them. Why did they do that? It seemingly served no practical purpose. Were they mimicking the wind, or did they imagine they could restore the object to

life by breathing into it? Once they heard a sound—our exha-
lation giving the object new life—even though the action was
fundamentally useless, they did it again and again, shaping it,
making it sound the way they wanted it to sound, time and
time again, rejecting, perfecting, imagining; and thousands of
years later, in 1847, a German named Theobald Böhm created
the modern flute. Presented at the London Exhibition of 1851,
it set the standard we have come to accept today, effectively
ending a journey of human discovery and development in
search of optimal beauty of tone and practicality that began
in the Stone Age.

Today's wind instruments are made of various materials:
different kinds of wood for oboes, clarinets, and bassoons; silver, platinum, and gold for flutes; and an alloy of copper and
zinc for the brass family. Imagine for a moment that once civilization learned the secrets of metallurgy and created bronze
from mixing copper with tin, humans used that technology
to make weapons, farming tools—and musical instruments.
Gold and bronze trumpets have been found in ancient Egyptian graves. The wind instruments made of metal were, and
are, so much louder than those made of wood. And while you
can see Egyptian paintings of flutelike and harplike instruments, consider the concept of a Roman army marching to
the piercing sounds of drums and brass as they conquered
much of the world, heralding their arrival from miles away.
It is what Cleopatra heard with the arrival of Julius Caesar,
and it is something we can experience today on Bastille Day
in Paris, or on Thanksgiving in Manhattan.

The history of percussion instruments is even easier to
imagine. Cutting wood into blocks that are the same width and
thickness but of different lengths makes a proto-xylophone.
Pythagoras demonstrated the mathematics of the pitch of a

vibrating object related to its length. Taking the skin of an animal and stretching it across a hollow circle of some kind makes the drum family: the bigger the circle, the deeper the sound. With the discovery of bronze, a great variety of bells, gongs, and cymbals demanded very specific tooling devices to achieve the precise sound the inventors and developers wanted, creating some of the most profound and reverberant wave forms of any instrument—a sound that came to mean the sanctity and mysteries of the church and the temple. We even expressed gratitude for the bounties of the earth by creating chimes that responded to the wind, thus letting Mother Nature's breath play an instrument humankind had invented.

You might also wonder at the development of the keyboard for pianos, harpsichords, organs, and celestas. Making use of the shape and size of the human hand and the desire to play more than one note at a time, the keyboard solved the problem—but required the technology to get a note from the depressing of a key to an actual sound. Consider for a moment how that challenge was met. (Strike a note on a pipe organ and somehow a specific pipe—or set of pipes—sounds from a great distance, wind blowing through the pipe that is turned on and off by that single key.)

Last among the families are the instruments that depend on a vibrating string made from the small intestines of a mammal, twisted and stretched across two points and made to vibrate either by plucking it with a finger or by drawing a bow across it, the latter constructed from the rough hair of a horse's tail—made rougher still by applying pine resin to the hair—and all made to sound louder by placing the string over a hollow wooden box. In other words: a violin! That small intestine might have been something useful, like the casing on a sausage, instead of an A string. Consider for a moment how many thousands of years of human interaction with animals and plants went into creating the violins, violas, cellos, and basses, and then regard the entire symphony orchestra, warming up before you: this miracle of technology and vast cultural history that we have achieved together in collaboration with the planet we have come to know and inhabit. These truly are the songs of the earth. And that does not even begin our reflection on the music composed for the instruments and the people who have devoted their lives to the perfection of playing them.

Music is as much a part of being human as anything we know of humanity. You may feel inclined to say, "I don't know anything about music," but in fact you know everything you need to know about music, even if you don't have technical words to describe your experiences with it. If you do not like it, that is perfectly okay. If you are curious about it, there are many ways to proceed on a journey of discovery that will reward you for the rest of your life.

The language of Western music, rather than the instruments we play it on, is heard from the first moment you were aware of your mother humming before you were born. Every children's song, every soundtrack, every encounter with music is an experience with this language. The meaning of its metaphors is taught to you all the time. You know its language of emotions, how you feel when you hear a fanfare on trumpets, a sentimental violin solo, and the approach of danger signaled by pulsing lower strings and a bass drum. Every day more and more understanding is added to your dictionary—one that is commonly shared by everyone who hears Western music. Above all, the worldwide popularity of motion pictures with their symphonic underscoring has taught the world the meaning of Western music, whether or not you grew up in Europe, where practically all of its formative composers received their training.

This is music that is easy to understand once you agree to open yourself to it, even when the jargon can be confusing and off-putting (an octave has not eight but twelve notes in it!). But the jargon is an attempt to translate music (which is invisible) into nouns and verbs and the descriptive words that modify them. Experiencing music is fundamentally emotional, after all, and it was composed for people to listen to and enjoy. Some of it was composed for you to play in your homes with your friends and family, but in our time chamber music has become a lost societal art. Instead, we have recordings and broadcasts heard on personal devices, thus cutting society out of the listening experience and replacing it with a direct connection to you, going as far as eliminating all the other sounds that exist outside your noise-canceling earbuds. At the same time, it makes live performance, in which we participate as an audience with other humans, all the more precious and essential, as we shall discuss later.

Because Western music is a uniquely descriptive and narrative language, it is not surprising that many of the works in the standard repertory describe the natural world. When Ravel composed his sunrise at the beginning of part 3 of the ballet *Daphnis et Chloé* in 1912, he assumed that the long melody that builds in loudness, climbing upward from the lowest voices in the orchestra surrounded by swirls of rapid notes and capped by a wordless chorus on "ah," would be accepted, translated, and understood by your brain as representing in sound what your eyes see. That is not something you should take for granted. It is miraculous.

What makes it personal is when you first heard certain music, where you were, how much it affected you, and how it related to other things happening to you at the time. When I was ten years old, my uncle Jim showed off his new high-fidelity sound system with a recording of "Dawn" from *Daphnis et Chloé*. Right from its mysterious first moments, when Ravel presented my ears with two musical elements—the gentle whoosh of woodwinds and harps quietly undulating while a serpentine bass line slowly slithered up and down—I was drawn into a new acoustic land of epic wonderment. The songs of Broadway were, for me, a single thing: a singer with a relatively homogenous background of instruments to accompany him or her. Classical music from my parents' old 78s and the music coming from tiny speakers in our television set had a similar impact of condensing all music into a mid-range acoustical compromise. Now, for the first time, there was a separation between the rapid-fire notes from clarinets that were given a magical haze from harps—all in the middle of my hearing spectrum—and a melody from the bottom. Tweets and trills from solo instruments seemed to describe colorful exotic birds as the music got progressively louder until it reached a plateau of gentle loveliness.

Nothing, however, prepared me for the journey I was about to go on, because each plateau was followed by another one that was even more beautiful and even louder, until I thought the plateglass window overlooking uncle Jim's garden was sure to shatter.

It was the most beautiful music I had ever heard, and I will never forget the thrill of those five minutes. This was a dawn I had never seen, nor could I have imagined it until that afternoon. The sun had risen more than once, as if Ravel had described it from a great distance and repeated it again and again, each time bringing us closer to it until, Icarus-like, I practically melted from being so close to something so magnificent. Never before in my experience as a child had I known a story to be nonlinear. Classical music had, in one five-minute track on a high-fidelity demonstration disc, become something I wanted to pursue.

More than a half century later, I vividly remember the room and precisely where my brother sat, and I can re-create where I stood transfixed, leaning on the back of a chair in my uncle's living room in 1956.

Like the twelve thousand Londoners who flocked to Green Park to hear the dress rehearsal of Handel's *Royal Fireworks Music* in 1749, I did not need a master's degree in music to understand Ravel's dawn. In the mid-1700s Bach wrote for his parishioners in Leipzig who did not study music. Tchaikovsky had all of us in mind in 1888 and 1889 when he wrote *The Sleeping Beauty,* just as Prokofiev did when he wrote *Cinderella* in the early 1940s.

Music is a human invention, and understanding it emerges out of our shared nature in mimicry with the animal kingdom. Biologists, for example, have studied songbirds and how their brains are specially designed to find mates for life. When finches hatch, the father finch teaches the male chicks his mating song. They practice until they get it right, at which time they are ready to enter the outside world. When a young female finch is ready to procreate, she listens to various males who sing the songs of their fathers to her. When she hears the song she likes, she mates with that male finch and the two remain together for the rest of their lives.

Ornithologists like Richard O. Prum are investigating the subjective decisions made by birds. Are they based on aesthetics? Does the female make her decision based on what we would call "beauty"—beauty of sound or beauty of its construction and repetition of notes and rhythms? For whatever we might imagine, the female bird was hearing the songs as seductive metaphors for the quality of her potential suitors.

You should never be embarrassed to reject the music you just don't like. In a strange way, musicians (composers and performers) act as the male finch for you, the audience. When you like what we are performing, we have succeeded. We are all choosy. "I like Beethoven, but I don't like the way Maestro X conducts it," "Very lovely performance, but it certainly wasn't Mozart," "No one plays Liszt better than Z." In each case, the person is acting like the female finch. In this sense, communication in music mimics the basic communication and seduction skills of the animal kingdom.

Recent studies show that early humans and Neanderthals had a remarkable ability to create metaphors and symbols of our perceived world. Perhaps as far back as 200,000 years ago, our ancestors dealt with symbolic thought. We know that approximately 40,000 years ago our ancestors painted two-dimensional images on cave walls and understood those images as representing three-dimensional animals. When our early ancestors wanted to imply motion, they gave the animals extra legs.

With symbolic thought there is language. And since symbols and metaphors are a part of who we are, music and art are not something reserved for an intellectual elite. We can laugh when we hear that American mafia thugs brought to trial in New York referred to cash bribes as "ziti," but this same creative act is at the heart of all language, including music. Words stand for things, and those things can stand for other things. In this case, the use of two monosyllables, "cash" and "bribes," which are sounds referring to the concept of money and an illegal use of it for profit, are represented by a macaroni dish every Sicilian loves. So it is with the sounds of music: the instruments that play it, the harmonies that underscore it, the tempo of the work, and the kinds of melodic elements you are processing somehow combine to have a meaning for you.

Some may ask if the old adage that "music is the international language" is true, since the classical music people throughout the world have embraced was composed, as I said, by white male Europeans. Of course, certain peoples take a collective pride in claiming composers as "theirs." Part of the residue of the last century and its use of music as a fundamental element of cultural superiority is that Austro-Germans take pride in every note composed by Beethoven as if they had a unique racial/patriotic connection to his eternal genius—it is part of their identity. Does every Italian feel he or she "knows" how Verdi should be performed, as if there were something immutable in what it means to be Italian? This pride can be a national pride (Schoenberg saw himself as a savior of German music, and Wagner wrote an entire opera—*Die Meistersinger*—lauding German art), a regional pride (Bellini was Sicilian, *not* Italian, if you are a Sicilian), a racial pride (Miklós Rózsa saw himself as a Magyar as well as a Hungarian and an American citizen), and even a family pride (when Maxim Shostakovich conducts his father's music, it is difficult to challenge his interpretations, as was true with Siegfried Wagner—everyone else becomes an outsider). When I was conducting a program with the Israel Philharmonic by refugee composers who fled to the United States during World War II, a member of the orchestra asked me, "Are you Jewish?" It seemed to him unusual, and perhaps even suspicious, for a non-Jew to be interested in conducting "Jewish" music.

In this sense, each composer of classical music belongs to someone's group. The music is theirs, and we are outsiders. Yet, of course, since music belongs to everyone and depends on interpretation to exist, it is very possible that a so-called outsider could interpret classical music as personally and convincingly as anyone from the group that identifies with the composer. (We still generally adhere to the idea that a French conductor "knows" French music better than anyone else. This is true of Russian, American, German, and Italian repertory also. Just look at the names of the guest soloists visiting our greatest orchestras.) Music, however, is a sneaky immigrant and knows no borders.

There is common ground that supersedes the "nativism" of classical music. Leonard Bernstein demonstrated that reality when, as an American, from the mid-1940s on, he performed Europe's greatest classical compositions to worldwide adulation. Seiji Ozawa certainly proved the point in the 1960s and thereafter, as did Zubin Mehta. Classical music could be interpreted at the highest level by non-Caucasians and non-Europeans. Recordings of *Carmen* by the Englishman Sir Thomas Beecham, the Austrian Herbert von Karajan, and the American Leonard Bernstein remain as valid as the one conducted by the Frenchman Georges Prêtre.

Classical music is not a wall—it is a bridge. It is more like an ur-religion than an expression of any one country or race, and it can never be captured and delimited by nationalism. Beethoven belongs to everyone.

No matter where we grew up, we all affix meaning to the music we hear. In the nineteenth century, writers were describing Schumann's symphonies as "novels of feeling" (*Gefühlsnovelle*). The metaphors can be short: the ting of a triangle to describe the sudden arrival of an idea (eureka!). They can also be extended and combined into the ritual journey of an opera lasting many hours, filled with internal metaphors of various lengths and adding up to a profound composite artifact of human behavior. A relatively undramatic opera like Bizet's *Les Pêcheurs de Perles* is nonetheless a Christian parable of two men who love each other and who also love the same woman.

Each of these three characters has a solo aria and each couple has a duet, until one of the men fulfills a greater love by giving the other two to each other—even though it means he may face death. At every level, big and small, of this fairly simple work, we are experiencing a profound lesson told metaphorically through music.

You may wonder how the concept of music as metaphor works. After all, we refer to a figure of speech that represents an object or action as a metaphor. The most obvious metaphors in classical music derive from mimicry, or onomatopoeia. We laugh, cry, gasp in astonishment, and sigh—and music can do this, too, by imitating the sounds we make. The opening of Zoltán Kodály's 1926 opera *Háry János* is a musical imitation of a sneeze. Nature and life on earth are never quiet, and they are therefore perfect inspirations for imitation.

Recently the astrophysicist Alan Lightman wrote in *Searching for Stars on an Island in Maine* (2018): "If one listens, there is always music on this island. The waves rolling into the shore make cascades of sound, sometimes regular rhythms and sometimes duples and triples and offbeat syncopations— all set against the arpeggios and glissandos of the birds." The sounds made by storms, the whistling of wind in the trees, thunder, pummeling rain, and the rushing of waters all have been inspiration for a diverse group of our most beloved composers: Vivaldi (*The Four Seasons:* "Summer"), Rossini (the *William Tell* Overture), Beethoven (the *Pastoral* Symphony), Verdi (*Rigoletto*), Tchaikovsky (*The Tempest*), Wagner (*Der fliegende Holländer* and *Die Walküre*), Richard Strauss (the *Alpine* Symphony), Sibelius (*The Tempest*), Gershwin (*Porgy and Bess*), and Britten (*Peter Grimes*).

However, what do we mean by music as metaphor when the object to be described is silent but visible? When Wagner faced the challenge of composing a rainbow for the final scene of his

1854 *Das Rheingold,* he assumed the listeners would accept the
Greek principle that higher notes would be heard as actually
higher, in the sense of the rungs of a ladder being higher than
the ones below. He therefore created a musical metaphor in
which the melody traces the notes of a simple chord that go up
and then down, but each time the musical ascent starts again
it begins and ends one note higher, therefore metaphorically
expressing the different colors of the rainbow.

When composers wish to represent something that is not
associated with a sound or a specific object, music can still
express—and expand—its metaphorical power. Spring is
symbolic of music itself, since both exude a sense of constant
rebirth. Unlike tempests and sneezes, there is no sound to
mimic spring. Instead, composers have attempted to elicit the
feeling derived from spring, thus creating a less obvious challenge to invent potent metaphors. Spring has inspired compositions that span the entire period of the classical canon,
starting with Vivaldi's "Spring" from *The Four Seasons,* composed in 1723, and including compositions by Mendelssohn,
Schumann, Johann Strauss Jr., Grieg, and Debussy, and ending with a rather unexpected one by Stravinsky in 1913, *The
Rite of Spring.* (The composer famously pointed out that in
Russia, after the deep freeze of winter, spring arrives with a
crack.)

The metaphorical lexicon of Western music came to
include musical evocations of death (Mozart's *Don Giovanni,*
various scenes in Verdi and Wagner, symphonic works by
Richard Strauss, Tchaikovsky, Sibelius, Shostakovich, and
Mahler), faith, humor (first perfected by Haydn), joy, love
(both spiritual and carnal, the latter invented by Wagner in
Tannhäuser)—and even complex emotions such as regret,
loneliness, fear, sarcasm, and foolishness (Wagner's musical
depiction of a music critic in *Die Meistersinger* and Haydn's

musical description of a doddering old fool in the finale to his Symphony no. 60, *Il distratto*). All of this has been created through the use of notes, harmonies, and orchestration, built within the simple framework of the basic rules and conventions of classical music.

When a composer tells us what the work is about (a symphony by Beethoven is not simply called no. 6 but has a title: *Pastoral*), we will imagine the sounds as specifically descriptive of its title. If you are hearing that same composer's subsequent symphony, simply called no. 7, you are on your own. When you encounter a movement of a symphony with the title Andante, you might know that this word means "walking speed" and refers to something people regularly did (and do), which is take a walk, usually in nature. Beethoven, for example, did this every day after lunch, carrying notepaper with him. Mahler composed his symphonies during the summer and inevitably in a cottage away from city life in Vienna and New York, taking walks and translating the scents, the sights, and the feelings that he derived from being with and of nature. Wagner climbed mountains, hiked through forests, into storms, and through the clouds in Switzerland so he could find inspiration for the musical metaphors that pervade his *Ring* Cycle: earth, fire, and water imbue huge swaths of his epic score.

A walk in nature along a well-trodden path—or perhaps a new one—will be filled with thoughts, memories, and discoveries. A sudden *fortissimo* interrupting a very quiet walk in the Andante movement of Haydn's Symphony no. 94 is the surprise in the well-known *Surprise* Symphony. Andante movements can also provide the most emotional experiences in a symphony—provided you open yourself to the journey, for then *you* become the walker.

The Andante that takes me into the most precious and intimate place is the second movement of Brahms's Symphony no. 3. Its opening melody is played on the solo clarinet, which is then followed by a mysteriously empathetic echo, led by the cellos. Pastoral music ensues as we continue on our way. The clarinet seems to be the walker. The echoes are shadows of something profound. Joy and sorrow are presented in an admixture of beauty. After six and a half minutes, the shadow reveals itself in a new melody from somewhere else. What is that song? Even if you do not know, it rises to epic heights before stopping abruptly, the harmonies unsettled, as if asking for directions. "Do I go this way or that? I have lost my sense of direction in the woods." Ultimately the walkers—that is, Brahms, you, and I—find our way back to the home key: a radiant halo of C major. That, in and of itself, is sufficient to experience the greatness of this movement within the symphony.

If, however, you recognize that new melody as being a leitmotif associated with love in Wagner's *Ring*—first articulated by Sieglinde in her love scene with Siegmund with the words *"Du bist der Lenz"* ("You are the spring")—and know that Wagner died while Brahms was composing this symphony, this walk in the forest has a shattering effect. The surviving composer, who owned manuscripts from the music of his presumed archrival, is ruminating on life and death and honoring Wagner's immense achievement while mourning the loss of a colleague, not an enemy. And if that isn't enough, the implicit lesson then becomes personal and contemporary: as any walk in the forest will teach you, we are all colleagues, intertwined earth creatures trying our best to survive and always knowing that our time here is finite and precious.

CHAPTER 4

Time: Real and Imaginary

Albert Einstein playing the violin on the S.S. *Belgenland*,
en route to California in 1931

Throughout history, humans have been preoccupied with the concept of time—how we experience it, how to measure it, how to establish synchronicity, and how to make use of it. From Stonehenge to whatever timepiece you use to determine what time it is right now, measuring it was done through observing cycles. Obviously, we see dawn every day. We can observe how the sun changes its point of arrival at the horizon, moving slightly every morning in one direction and then back again, only to repeat that action about 365 mornings later. The clock and the calendar became external predictors and explainers. Internally, we observed our need to sleep in the dark and rise in the daylight, and we used memory to predict and prepare. It took until 1884 to invent the International Date Line—a most vexing necessity in our time-obsessed world—and thus join the clock to the calendar.

In spite of all our machinations, time remains a mystery. Is it an invention? A convenience? Is it real? While these questions may seem beside the point, they are precisely the point in attempting to understand the effect music has on us. In 1882, Richard Wagner in *Parsifal* used an extraordinary poetic image, when an aged knight of the Holy Grail explains to a young innocent who feels that he is not walking and yet is unwittingly traveling toward an eternal sacred object: that "time here becomes space" ("Du siehst, mein Sohn, zum Raum wird hier die Zeit"). An early-twentieth-century amateur musician who surely would have known Wagner's final masterpiece went on to prove it by using the most famous equation ever presented, one that we all know but few of us really understand: $E = mc^2$.

To this day, physicists and philosophers continue their fascination with time and a thing we all call "reality." The problem is that we perceive reality from being in it, agreeing (more or less) on what it is. Physicists are trying to establish the concept from the outside—not a simple matter. In fact, there are those who believe it is impossible to determine the truth of anything from inside it, but equally impossible to escape from its confines and, godlike, describe cosmic machinery from the outside. Can advanced physics—mathematics, after all—pierce the membrane of our limited perceptions? Perhaps the universe itself is merely a hologram or a computer simulation, as Stephen Hawking and others have suggested.

You might well ask, Why should that matter? If reality exists beyond our senses, and nothing is what it seems, we can then create our own reality, our own belief systems, and find comfort in the chaos by imprinting a reasonably good explanation for everything around and inside us. After all, the concept of the atom existed for centuries, starting with the ancient Greeks, and it was a "useful construct" until the aforementioned amateur musician, Albert Einstein, offered a theoretical proof in 1905. Music turns out to be inextricably involved with time, acting as a very useful construct.

It should be said that music plays with different *kinds* of time. Obviously, there's the chronological, or durational, time: how long—in terms of the clock—does a piece of music last? There's historical time: when was it written? There's emotional time: how long did it feel like? There's personal time: when did I first hear this work, and how does my memory link that time and each successive time to where I am now?

All of the above is not inconsiderable, and accounts for a central mystery—and attraction—of all music, but especially classical music, because of its multiple uses of time and mem-

ory. Works of tremendous profundity can be quite short, like
Rachmaninoff's Vocalise, or the intermezzo from Mascagni's
Cavalleria rusticana—a mere three and a half minutes. Both
works exude a kind of time suspension that casts a spell and
makes brevity irrelevant to their exquisite and sad beauty.
On the other hand, orchestral concerts usually contain about
ninety minutes of music, with some works—like a Mahler
symphony—occasionally taking up the entire program. Members of the Metropolitan Opera Orchestra used the fact that
their colleagues across Lincoln Center Plaza who play in the
New York Philharmonic would be leaving their concert hall
for the night just as the Met players were returning to the pit
for act 2 of Wagner's *Götterdämmerung* as a bargaining tool for
greater pay. A performance of the opera requires about five
and a half hours from the first notes of its prologue to the final
curtain. The time commitment, it should be noted, is not just
for the orchestra. It's for all of us, too.

It comes as a real surprise to know that Beethoven's Fifth
Symphony is a mere twenty-six minutes long. Beethoven's
nine symphonies constitute the greatest sequence of symphonies ever composed. They take us on a journey of tradition and transition from the courtly music of Haydn, who, as
already noted, created the symphonic structure, to expanding
the form into unprecedented levels of emotion, length, and
power. These symphonies, completed between 1801 and 1824,
are the epicenter of classical music and its symphonic traditions; and yet, if you were to decide right now to listen to all
nine Beethoven symphonies, it would take up approximately
six hours of your day, just a little longer than one opera by
Wagner.

We could argue that all art takes up time. Music, however,
not only demands our time to experience it: we are under its

control *in order* to experience it. You can speed-read an article or a book, skipping over things you choose to ignore. Plays can be produced in highly cut and edited forms—few have ever experienced a complete performance of *Hamlet*, even though it is Shakespeare's most famous play. And while it is true that you can play highlights from your favorite Mahler symphony, jumping to the recorded finale of his *Resurrection*, that is like being airlifted to the top of a mountain to take a selfie. You will not have earned it, and it will seem pretty but trivial. Music takes its time—and your time. Should you agree to enter its realm, it will control your sense of time until it releases you when the music has ended. In this sense, classical music is both of its time, in its time, and completely timeless. Once we give in to the control of the composer and his trans-lators, our sense of real time is suspended.

Historical time is another part of the story. Every piece of music represents some aspect of the time and place of its composition, and possibly (this is controversial) the emo-tional state of the composer when it was written. Obviously it is possible for a sad composer to write happy music, and we cannot always assume that music expresses the state of mind of its author. That said, it is generally unusual for this to hap-pen. The death of Mozart's father just before he composed *Don Giovanni*, which is after all about the death of a father, imbues the arias and ensembles of that masterpiece, and lis-teners would do well to carefully listen to the many times an inner line or a melodic phrase outlines a descending chromatic scale (i.e., utilizing all the white and black notes found on a keyboard). Even the happy music in the opera contains this river of grief within it. Since we hear music in terms of up and down, the downward pull of these shadow melodies registers as a powerful commentary, even when they are subliminal.

Stravinsky, who presented himself as an unemotional intellectual leader in the music of his century, composed his Symphony in C during a time of terrible personal strife. In 1937 he was diagnosed with tuberculosis, which later claimed the lives of his wife and a daughter. In 1939, his mother passed away. The composer wrote the first two movements in Europe, the third movement in Cambridge, Massachusetts—having emigrated to the United States due to World War II—and the fourth movement in Hollywood. Listening to this work, you would be challenged to hear his personal life in the notes he composed, and the composer insisted on that interpretation of emotional detachment between his life and his music.

On the other hand, once he settled in West Hollywood— the city that would become his home for longer than any place in the world—he composed his Symphony in Three Movements, completed in 1945. The composer referred to this symphony as his "war symphony." In his 1962 book, *Dialogues and a Diary* (written with Robert Craft), Stravinsky stated that the first movement was a musical response to a documentary he had seen that exposed the brutal Japanese scorched-earth policy in China. The last movement was inspired by films showing Nazi soldiers goose-stepping, and the work's surprising ending—a half-step higher than, as the composer said, "the expected C"—in some way "tokens my extra exuberance in the Allied triumph." Then, as if to counter his very personal admission of how and why the symphony was composed, Stravinsky said, "But enough of this. In spite of what I have said, the Symphony is not programmatic. Composers combine notes. That is all. How and in what form the things of this world are impressed upon their music is not for them to say."

The above quotation sums up the philosophical position

that music is without inherent meaning and that we, the listeners, impress ideas and feelings upon it. It is a strong current of thought that runs through the twentieth century and into our own. However, since we might agree that it is the listener who will decide what music might mean, Stravinsky wants to have it both ways. He simply writes notes and we apply whatever stories we want onto them, even as he has given us an insight as to what inspired those notes in the first place.

When we want to know more about a classical work, we inevitably feel there will be some relationship between the composers' histories and the notes that come from them, even when they are the opposite of what we might expect. Composers (as in the case above) may disagree, but actually it is out of their hands once their music is released and published. Any listener who plays a recording of the Symphony in C and follows it immediately with the Symphony in Three Movements will hear the differences and the similarities between the two works. I always find the emotional detachment in the earlier symphony to be as moving as the passionate thrust of the latter, when the composer was safe and forging a new life. We musicians know that in times of deepest sadness we can always return to "the air we breathe," to borrow a phrase from Arnold Schoenberg. Music is our comfort and our companion no matter what. As his world—indeed, his life—seemed to be passing away before him in 1938, Stravinsky composed a perfectly balanced and classically structured symphony in a remarkably twentieth-century idiom. Mahler would have been weeping and composing vast funeral marches, but not Stravinsky. Music protected him by his entering a place of cool detachment and civility—a modern reflection of the courtly lives of Haydn and Mozart was his shield and his armor.

The latter work, the Symphony in Three Movements, carries a level of raw emotion and drama that is closer to the early Stravinsky, the Stravinsky of *The Firebird* and *The Rite of Spring*. Some of its musical elements were drawn from a film project that Stravinsky abandoned (music for an adaptation of Franz Werfel's *The Song of Bernadette*) and, as the composer said, were also inspired by documentary films of World War II. It has another, very personal significance for me. It is the music of my birth year.

I have become fascinated with the classical music composed around the time of my birth in 1945: music by Bartók, Shostakovich, Stravinsky, Prokofiev, Copland, Bernstein, Schoenberg, Hindemith, Richard Strauss, Korngold, and Britten. Their compositions somehow embody the world into which I was born, and I am proud to have existed when those composers were alive and writing new music. I find learning about the history of classical music—the political landscape; what was simultaneously happening in the arts; indeed, whatever I can find to conjure a time and place of an imagined historical environment—to be one of the major elements in deconstructing a work of classical music. I do understand that this is a profoundly personal process, but it is one that every person who loves classical music might wish to follow, and probably, unknowingly, already does.

When I learned that Mahler composed his Symphony no. 5 from the inside out, suddenly everything made sense to me. The immense middle movement—its Scherzo—was the first to be composed in 1901. The implications of this stand-alone movement told the composer what to do with it to turn it into a symphony. My journey into the most rudimentary understanding of why one note follows the other began with this knowledge. Beethoven was already waging an internal battle to transcend his progressive hearing loss as Napoleon was conquering Europe (the audience for the world premiere of his opera *Leonore*—before he turned it into *Fidelio*—consisted largely of French soldiers stationed in Vienna); Ravel's devastating experiences behind the lines in World War I informed the nightmarish endings to his *La Valse* and *Boléro* and the entirety of his Concerto for the Left Hand; a stop at a piano shop in Paris during Tchaikovsky's 1891 journey to New York to open Carnegie Hall resulted in his discovery of the magical sound of the celesta, which he then used to depict the Sugar Plum Fairy in his as-yet-unfinished ballet *The Nutcracker*.

As a New Yorker or a Parisian, you may want to "own" that bit of historical linkage—Tchaikovsky/Mustel's piano shop/Carnegie Hall/*The Nutcracker*—which creates the aura of a time before we lived, but which we can imagine. Americans, for example, might find it interesting to learn that Benjamin Franklin, who spent over twenty-eight years as a representative of the American colonies in England and France, attended a London performance of *Messiah* conducted by the composer eight days before Handel's death in 1759. Henry Ford, it is said, traveled from Detroit to Munich in 1910 to attend the world premiere of Mahler's Symphony no. 8. The breath and breadth of history empowers classical music and invites us to live in an imaginary historical time, should we choose to.

History, like time, is a construct. In 1761, Haydn entered the employ of one of the richest and most influential families in Europe, the Esterházys, in Eisenstadt, Austria. For thirty years Haydn was free to invent and compose for the court; and "cut off from the world," as he wrote, "I was forced to become original." Haydn's music for Count Esterházy can make us feel as if we are a member of the court, but without all the other accoutrements, dangers, and inconveniences of its time:

a pretend castle of the mind with indoor plumbing and central heating. And if you are unable to visit the castle, which is now a museum, you can at least look up photographs of it to inspire your imagination, should you choose to. On the other hand, you can simply listen to his music.

It is part of its legacy that classical music represents an idealized civilization. Instrumental ensembles are by their nature an idealized community, since every player is dependent on the others in order to play together as a unified ensemble. In some cases, classical music carries within it the civilization of the time and place of the composition. In other cases, it is an imagined evocation of a time and civilization that *preceded* the music's composition. No one knows what ancient Egyptian music sounded like, but when Verdi invented an effective musical metaphor for it—using exotic scales and a primary place for harps and flutes in his 1870 *Aïda*—the world accepted it as authentic enough. This music created a romanticized and essentially "fake" Egyptian sound that is also a very real echo of how people in the late nineteenth century co-created ancient Egypt, when exoticism was rampant in Europe. In this same way, a newly imagined Egyptian sound that made use of studies in ethnomusicology and jazz was persuasively fantasized by Alex North in his 1963 score to the motion picture *Cleopatra*, and three years later in Samuel Barber's music to the opera *Antony and Cleopatra*.

Music can and does underscore our nostalgia for an idealized past, but because it is not a visual medium, it manages to transcend embarrassing accuracy, substituting an ambiguity that requires you to cocreate its images. Cocreation brings a sense of ownership, as many lovers of classical music will demonstrate in the passion they express for it. In that sense, the fake is made true by a coconstructed narrative. The audi-

ence is always the ultimate translator of music. Patricia Vigderman, in her book *The Real Life of the Parthenon* (Ohio State
University Press, 2018), rightly says, "The past is . . . in need
of the present's care and memory in order for it to have meaning and worth."

Since historians can choose where to begin and where
to end their stories, Hayden White invented the word
"emplotment"—meaning the imprint of dramatic structure
onto what he saw as the randomness of events. "Even the most
basic beginning-middle-end structure represents an imposi-
tion." For him, the middle of the story is the most question-
able because the historian inevitably decides what is important
once the curtain has gone up on the drama called "history."

Of course, we could say that about every story, history or
not. The first sentence and the last are the constructs—the
original sin, if you will. "Once upon a time . . . They all lived
happily ever after." Everything in between is transition or
process. In this sense, music is itself a history in the way its
composers capture time, manipulating it for you to accept as
some kind of truth about human experience. Everyone knows
the opening of Beethoven's Fifth Symphony. Beethoven takes
those four notes, G–G–G–E-flat, and starts us on a journey
based on how he processes that motif. It builds, returns, stops,
and interrupts until it finally returns to conclude the first movement. It then makes a surprising return later in other movements, as if it is some kind of inevitable force—and it becomes
that force because of the way Beethoven uses it, adapts it, and
makes use of your memory to perceive its journey throughout
a symphony with no words and no name other than a number.
It becomes a truth of how humans think and process information. And when we arrive at the last movement, and the key
of the symphony—which had been firmly established to be

in the minor mode—abruptly becomes C major, we all feel
the triumph of the idea. Beethoven loads his deck by adding
instruments that have remained mute until that moment: a piccolo, a contrabassoon, and three trombones expose a larger
universe waiting for discovery. And yes, at its conclusion,
Beethoven projects a world of "happily ever after" in the language of music.

It has been argued that our sense of time is based on two
things: memory and expectation. In other words, we can only
project what will come based on what has happened. This idea
removes "now" from the concept of time. We conductors are
always dealing with what was just played so as to shape what
is about to be played. The now of music dissolves into the past
so quickly that it may be irrelevant to any conception of time.
That said, memory is probably the strongest element in our
relationship to classical music and the pleasure derived from
listening to it.

"We are the world's memories" is an evocative line from
Game of Thrones. In a way, the same can be said of music. Perhaps more relevant is that music is a compendium of memories. Music that impresses you on first hearing will stamp a
time clock on your life. Every subsequent hearing of this
music will be added to your experiential list, and also return
you to that first time.

Psychologists have pointed out that this is especially true of
music you love during adolescence and the awakening of your
adult self. Classical music is, after all, a very adult art form.
Its symbols and descriptions are frequently sexual; and like
romantic love, the music expressing these emotions doesn't
always make sense. It can be onomatopoetic (the *Tannhäuser*
Overture and the prelude to *Der Rosenkavalier*), and yet it is
never pornographic, because it is sound without a graphic con-

tent. One could call it porno-acoustic, and there are no laws against that. Sexual music is (oxymoronically) metaphorically realistic. In both examples cited above, it is significant that the music is played before a closed curtain, after which we observe a scene. The end of act 1 of Wagner's *Die Walküre* describes the sexual congress of Siegmund and Sieglinde, an action that breaks two moral laws, since she is a married woman *and* the two characters are brother and sister.

Whenever you see this onstage, the director will inevitably have the couple look happy and run enthusiastically out the door into burgeoning spring, as Wagner's orchestra pulses in ever-accelerating pounding rhythms, culminating in an immense cadence. Wagner's stage description is quite different. "He draws her to him with passionate fervor; she falls on his chest with a scream. The curtain falls quickly." Indeed, what follows must be out of sight, offstage, or, in the Latin word for actions that are unacceptable to be viewed, *obscena*, from which we coined our word "obscene." Wagner conflates the time for the completed sexual act into approximately forty-five seconds. This suits his dramatic purpose, and no one would question its "reality." That said, in his opera *Tristan und Isolde* the love scene takes forty-five minutes before it reaches its climax. Unlike the conclusion of act 1 of *Die Walküre*, the *Tristan* lovemaking acts as the anchor not only for the second act but for the entire opera.

Preadolescents can of course listen to the most adult-themed classical music and not understand its specific intent. They will hear dramatically swirling melodies and throbbing rhythms. If they are attracted to what they have heard, their understanding will only increase as years pass by. As a boy, I heard the overture to Wagner's *The Flying Dutchman* as the theme music for a science-fiction television show called *Cap-*

tain Video, and it was absolutely thrilling. Only later in life did I learn it was music that described a supernatural storm that tossed a ghost across endless seas in the hopes of finding a woman who would love him and break the curse of his eternal wandering. When I first conducted the opera, the first imprint of the music to *Captain Video* was somewhere in the farthest reaches of my mind, but instead of it being heroic music, I knew its very first notes were a scream of the undead stranger for whom only death through true love was the goal. The notes were the same, but I certainly was not.

The inadvertent exposure to classical music in my youth came from many sources. Television, like movies, started out by culling classical music to announce its dramas before hiring composers to write new music for them. It was on television, as a child, that I first heard a vast embrace of classical music as the opening music for science, interview, news, drama, and puppet shows. Copland's *Billy the Kid,* Debussy's mysterious *Syrinx* for solo flute, Grieg's sentimental "Last Spring," and the Russian Dance from *The Nutcracker* were just a few works that shaped my knowledge of the glorious repertory that awaited me. Someone who produced *Captain Video* knew the music of Wagner and chose *Dutchman,* and it would not be the last time Wagner's descriptive music would underscore my childhood. The question you might be asking is "Does it happen today?"

That question was answered in the summer of 2018, when my two great-nephews (eight-year-old twins) were playing with Legos—the construction game that uses interlocking plastic blocks. One of them had successfully completed a task and began singing the "Hallelujah" Chorus from Handel's *Messiah.* The other joined in, singing in innocent merriment. They kept going well into the more complex development of the simple melodies, but the words were different. "What's that?" I asked. The answer: *"Captain Underpants!!!!"* A time will come when they hear a performance of Handel's *Messiah*, when vague memories of their youth are transformed and connected to classical music intended to celebrate the resurrection of Jesus. Nevertheless, two boys born in 2010 absolutely knew that a composition from 1741 was and continues to be music of triumph and joy.

In this way, music's invisibility makes it open to a much larger audience than graphic art. Posters advertising an exhibit of the erotically charged figurative art of Egon Schiele (1890–1918) were banned from public display in both Vienna and Britain in 2017. In defending the ads, Norbert Kettner of the Vienna Tourist Board was quoted as saying, "We want to show people just how far ahead of their time [the] protagonists [of Viennese modernism] really were." Perhaps one could say that the general public in any time might consider a large poster of a naked woman with her legs spread and directed at the viewer from the side of a bus was not "ahead of its time." Schiele was part of an era of provocation, and it would be hard to imagine what time he was ahead of, at least when it comes to public displays. Waiting for this aspect of modernism's conquest will be a long wait indeed—some time after the arrival of Godot, I would imagine. Music of that period, however, cannot be pasted on a bus or hung on a wall. The theater of the mind is and always will be the most important, private, protected, and effective. Bartók's suite from *The Miraculous Mandarin* is exciting and mysterious music when played in a concert. The ballet, if graphically presented, would be equivalent to Schiele's gritty and purposefully confrontational visions of moral decay.

There will be works that, once discovered, may journey

with you to the end of your time on earth. These are the works that comfort and return you to the time when you first encountered them. And, while performances will always keep them alive and unique, the works themselves will somehow remain and your long experience with them will be a measure of how you have changed and evolved. It is a window into personal gnosis—self-knowledge. It will generally tell you a story, both oft told and always morphing. On the other hand, classical music may merely keep you company.

Because I have been listening to and participating in classical music for over sixty years, every work I know is attached, as if by invisible strings, to some starting point, which in some cases is my childhood. You might think of this when choosing a gift for a child you care about. I still have my first recording of a classical work, Rimsky-Korsakov's *Scheherazade*, a Christmas gift to her young nephew from Aunt Marie. It is no accident that *Scheherazade* was the first big orchestral work I ever conducted as a student and that I subsequently recorded, at Abbey Road Studios, a decade later. When I first heard *The Rite of Spring*, I was fourteen years old, and I found it to be a terrific emotional experience—perfectly attuned to adolescent hormones—with the aged Stravinsky conducting it on a brand-new recording. Eight years later, I studied it from the score and conducted it for the first time. This was a shock, because I never knew that each section of it had an internal title. It was a story ballet!

The experience of that first performance in 1970 (with the Yale Symphony) of *The Rite* was titanic for me, and I exhibited anger for days afterward. That mystified me. When I was twenty-seven, I conducted it at my professional orchestral debut concert (with the Los Angeles Philharmonic). Again, it was thrilling but made me uneasy afterward. Finally, after a concert with the London Symphony Orchestra that consisted of *Scheherazade* and *The Rite of Spring,* I put *The Rite* away, never to conduct it again because of the story it tells and what I had to become in order to tell it. *The Rite of Spring* remains the same. Who I am and what I want to be is my story embedded within memories of that masterpiece of indifferent and effective violence. When I hear my colleagues perform it, I listen with curious detachment to see what it means to the maestro, the audience, and, of course, to me. I always come away in awe of its power and originality, but then I side with Stravinsky himself, who never went there again as a composer, because he knew what he had written.

Each new experience with music you know becomes part of your life, and as time moves on, it is added to your story— your history—like olfactory memories of Grandma's cooking, the smell of a newspaper, the paint for your model plane, your kindergarten teacher's perfume. Opera lovers may tell you of their first *La Bohème* and reminisce about each subsequent one: their age, whom they were with, what they thought, and who sang, even though classical music remains indifferent to how you interpret it and when you come to it. Those works admitted into the central repertory have become timeless, though you may recall the first time you acknowledged them. From then on, the music persists.

Because music acts as a life partner and is somehow inextricably attached to our memories, it is no surprise that it is being employed in geriatric as well as posttraumatic therapies. People suffering from impaired brain function can recapture themselves through music. The impaired brain can better deal with its handicaps when music creates an ambiguous but palpable matrix of order. Music maintains a form of coherence for the current self, as well as a time machine back to before.

The same is true for those suffering from physical ailments. Therapists will frequently play music to create a passageway to a time when a patient was able-bodied. The most moving experiences in my conducting career occurred when I went out into the audience after a performance at the Hollywood Bowl—at the request of families—to meet various terminally ill people. One woman said to me, "You made me feel like I can walk again." It was not I, of course. It was the music. But as its messenger, I could imagine no greater purpose in my life.

Your relationship with music will, and must, change during your life. After all, life experience gives you more reference points for connectivity. For scientists, this could also be related to the changes in our brain function and hearing. For religious people, it is like their ever-evolving relationship with God, and in a very real sense, our relationship with music is a relationship with an eternal and necessary unifying force. The Quakers believe that "there is that of God in each of us." Music's metaphors directly relate to the very concept of belief—a belief that there is something bigger than what we see and hear, a belief in an overriding structure of the invisible, and a sense of belonging to a race of sentient beings with a commonality that can otherwise be elusive. That commonality is not only with other humans but with nature itself: the physical universe of both known and unknown properties supported by our collective and extraordinary imagination.

CHAPTER 5

Invisible Structures

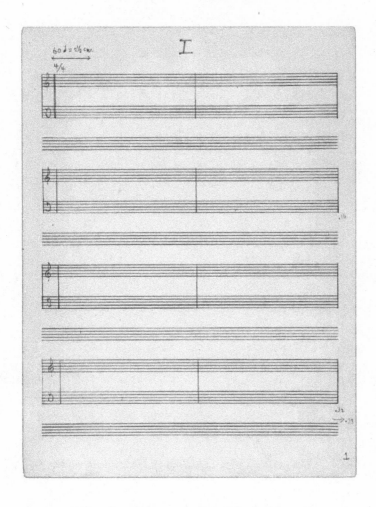

Manuscript of movement 1 from John Cage's *4:33*

Whenever someone wants to persuade you to love music by writing about it, the "proof" sometimes comes in some form of structural analysis: an intellectual pursuit justifying what is essentially an emotional response. The tools used to describe structure usually have to do with the relationship of keys and melodic (pitch) elements, and how they are deployed and developed to make a satisfactory construction. For those of us who read music, this can be really interesting, like delving into the mind of a composer who consciously or unconsciously created structural underpinning to his works, especially when it comes to music from the German tradition. But what if you can't hear them, or don't even subscribe to the idea that they are of significant importance in determining whether you like the piece or not?

When I was a freshman in college I learned how musicologists and music theorists analyze classical music, something that had never occurred to me. For eight years I had been going to the Metropolitan Opera regularly, listening to new and old classical music with friends, and attending concerts as well as Broadway musicals. Structure? Imagine my surprise to delve into a Bach cantata and a Haydn string quartet to see what made them tick. Classical music was becoming a puzzle to be solved—a pursuit of the mechanisms that were at play when a composer made music in long forms. Our eyes, staring at our miniature scores, were teaching our ears to hear what might not have been obvious. On the page we could see a melody move from a violin to a viola and then to a cello. We could see the structural repeats, because there was a repeat sign on the page. With ever-increasing insight into how composers construct music, we were like kids with Rubik's Cubes, taking the music apart and putting it back together again. As a student composer, all of this prepared me for the various ways to get from the first note to the last. As a conductor, it has served me well in getting inside the machine itself. The question will always remain as to whether an untutored listener is at a disadvantage in not having this training when hearing music. Do you need to be able to take apart and rebuild your toaster in order to enjoy the toast it makes?

By the time I was learning the rules of counterpoint and harmonic progression at Yale, I already had, to name just a few, two complete recordings of Beethoven's nine symphonies, Wanda Landowska's complete *Well-Tempered Clavier* of Bach (on six LPs), three recordings of *Aïda*, every new work recorded by Stravinsky, and one live recording from Bayreuth of *Parsifal* (also on six LPs)—all bought with money I earned mowing the lawn, painting the house, and babysitting. I had given lectures in high school on Wagner's *Ring* Cycle, Strauss's *Elektra*, and the history of French opera, and I am sure structure never came into my thinking at all, though it is a source of both approbation and severe criticism in academic music.

The first movement of Tchaikovsky's beloved Piano Concerto no. 1 was considered a disaster by a number of conservatory professors, starting with his Berlin-trained mentor, Nikolai Rubinstein, for structural as well as technical reasons—the principal one being that the opening is in the "wrong" key, D-flat major, for a work ostensibly in B-flat minor. When you listen next to this movement, notice that the famous opening melody is heard only twice and never again.

Instead, Tchaikovsky moves onward in the "correct" key and the rest of the movement behaves the way most every first movement is built (see below). In other words, from a structural point of view, the first four minutes of the concerto are an oversized introduction (in the wrong key) before the main event: the exposition. Some music theorists have done very creative backflips to prove the subtle relationship of that big and beloved tune with the rest of the concerto, but it is doubtful anyone hears it or, more importantly, cares. At its 1875 world premiere, the tradition-minded Bostonians responded to the new work with unbridled enthusiasm. Tchaikovsky, wounded by the scathing criticism from his mentor in Russia, gave the concerto and its world premiere to the Austrian Hans von Bülow to play on tour in the United States and thereby distance himself from any potential public humiliation. The premiere was a sensation, and the audience demanded that the last movement be repeated. (Humiliation was meted out by one of Boston's critics who famously wrote that the concerto "was hardly destined to become classical.") As Tchaikovsky wrote during his trip to America in 1891, "I am a much bigger deal here than in Russia."

Because of classical music's ability to create sonic environments that change and develop throughout the duration of each piece, it could very well be that most listeners are less interested in the architecture of music and far more attracted to its narrative capabilities. In my experience, the great works do both.

It's fair to say that there are two kinds of structures: the ones composers use to get from here to there when writing, and the ones people experience when, free of the score, they simply hear the music—and of course, hearing is the point. When Arnold Schoenberg developed his system of composition using all twelve notes within the octave by creating a unique ordering of them for each new piece (and the procedures for using them), he found a method to create a consistent sound. But no one I have ever met can actually hear and replicate a twelve-tone row or perceive how it functions by listening. It is a structural device that is quite different from, say, building a piece out of a theme and variations.

But let's back up for a moment. What are structures in sound? We could say that they are like invisible houses made of vibrating air and experienced through time. Are they important to the way we appreciate music? They certainly can be. If structures are building blocks, are they less important when a classical work is narrative rather than a kind of solved aural puzzle? In other words, is structure more important in a Bach fugue than in a Mahler symphony?

That is much harder to answer. I doubt anyone who loves Mahler is thrilled because of his creative use of the sonata form or the key relationships between the first and last movements. It may have a subliminal effect, mind you, but that would be a guess. After all, who knows what's going on in your mind as you are hearing a seventy-minute-long symphony?

Structures and procedures, however, are essential in *creating* long-form classical music. It is how composers stretch melodic ideas into whole movements, and sometimes whole symphonies. Hector Berlioz, for instance, came up with the concept of an *idée fixe*—a melody that keeps returning (among other melodies) within his *Symphonie fantastique*. It gives us a sense of continuity and comprehensibility. That little, and memorable, tune pops up in various guises throughout the five movements of this brilliant and passionate work and also helped the composer find his way to write the piece in the first place: a programmatic symphony that describes in musical metaphors "an episode in the life of an artist" who is obsessed with something or someone ("a beloved image"). It is a fact that Berlioz had fallen in love with the Irish actress Harriet Smithson, whom he saw play Ophelia in Paris in 1827. Having written to her many times, and to no avail, he composed his symphony about obsession, which premiered in 1830. (She did not attend.) But they did eventually meet and were married in 1833; Berlioz soon found out that reality and fantasy were two very different things. Nonetheless, the fact that an audience can also participate in Berlioz's structural device of a recurring *idée fixe* allows us to "understand" the notes being performed.

When Richard Strauss set out to write a series of tone poems, he took pre-existing traditional structures (created by other composers) to act as the framework for his narratives. It is as if he had it both ways: each work has a title and a story, but is built firmly on tried and true procedures of predecessors who were not composing works with story titles. (We will discuss the dichotomy of "absolute" music and "program" music a bit later.) When you hear *Till Eulenspiegel's Merry Pranks* you might recognize it as a rondo, with a "refrain" that gives the work coherence that is free of its title and its overt story-line. *Ein Heldenleben* makes use of an extended sonata form, and *Don Quixote* has the subtitle of "fantastical variations on a theme of knightly character."

Whenever you look at a building you rarely think about what holds it up, or all the things that go into the feelings you get when you enter it. The obvious architectural triumph of Gothic cathedrals is a good example, where stone and glass were made to rise hundreds of feet into the air in an artistic and technical triumph: a metaphor of the power and majesty of God. The same is true of the invisible architecture of music. One of the many things that link architectural design with musical structures is that they both must be experienced through time. You, however, control the time spent in architectural spaces, whereas music controls your time. Music never simply is: it is always *becoming*. Inevitably it also shares a resemblance to storytelling, even when it is called "Symphony no. 2" or "op. 27."

In a curious way, the music of the central canon shows both a structural integrity and a narrative capacity. The masterpieces are well-told tales. The first lesson I ever received from Leonard Bernstein was his belief that all the great works were built on a single tempo out of which all tempos are related. In other words, every movement of Handel's *Messiah* is based on a single pulse, multiplied or divided, but always expressing the work's temporal spine. At a seminar with us young conductors, he asked a colleague, "What is the relationship between the slow introduction to *Till Eulenspiegel* and the allegro?" The answer was 2:1. The slow introduction (marked "leisurely"—*gemächlich*—by Strauss) should set up the tempo of the allegro ("very lively"—*sehr lebhaft*), which is precisely twice as fast as the opening. The listener might not be overtly aware of this, but according to Bernstein, it is the glue that holds the piece together.

Verdi composed his operas based on multiples and divisions of tempo. *Un ballo in maschera* has as its spine multiples of 40 beats per minute, with 80 and 160 acting as interim guideposts. Did he expect us conductors to observe them, or was it one of his methods to, as I said earlier, get from here to there? Because Verdi indicated tempo in both expressive words (*allegro giusto, andante*) and metronome marks ("quarter note = 66 [beats per minute]"), we musicians are given the feeling Verdi wished to express and the recipe for achieving it. It was not surprising when, after a speech I gave at New York University in 2001, an Italian scholar told me that the composer had also created the architectural specifications for the expansion of his home, the Villa Verdi, in Sant'Agata.

If you are unaware of the most common structures in classical music, they are pretty obvious once you learn what they are,
because you can hear them. The last movement of Beethoven's
Symphony no. 3, the *Eroica*, is a series of variations on the
theme that is played, after a brief and energetic introduction,
on pizzicato strings. Brahms lets you know right away what he
is up to by his title *Variations on a Theme by Haydn*. In every
case of encountering this structural procedure—theme and
variations—you can follow the creativity of the composer in
adapting the simple tune in a series of transformations. The
joy comes from remembering the original theme (usually presented a couple of times at the top) and measuring it against
each new iteration.

Memory is the key to perception of any musical structure.
In the case of Rachmaninoff's 1934 *Rhapsody on a Theme of
Paganini*, the variation that is world famous (no. 18) cannot
be perceived as such because it does not sound anything like
the original melody. It is registered by the brain as a new tune
in the middle of the piece. For this variation, the composer
took the original melody and turned it upside down. This is
called an inversion. In other words, every time the original
melody goes up, the inversion goes down the same amount,
and so forth. Inversion is something composers have used as
a way of inventing new melodies that are still part of the fundamental musical materials, but they rarely can be understood
when heard by the listener. It is doubtful that anyone cares, it
should be said.*

It is much like the word play known as anagrams. Leonard

---

* In Jerome Kern's score to his 1927 musical *Show Boat*, the melody that underscores
the words "Cotton Blossom" in the opening number is inverted to create the famous
melody for "Ol' Man River." Because it is short (four notes) and retains the same
rhythm, it is perceivable.

Bernstein, like his friend Stephen Sondheim, loved anagrams, because by reordering the same letters of any word, a completely different-sounding word is created. This is very much what a composer does with the same intervals in a melody. Change the order and you have a new tune, even though it is made up of the same elements. English is a particularly good language for this word game. The name "Cathy," for example, can be transformed into the word "yacht." Of his and Sondheim's *West Side Story*, Bernstein particularly liked taking "It's alarming how charming I feel," from the song "I Feel Pretty," and anagrammatizing one word so that the result is "It's marginal how charming I feel." Since most people are not literate in reading music, the general public cannot study the score to see how the composer makes use of inaudible structures, whereas everyone who is reading this book can marvel at the alchemy of anagrams. "Leonard Bernstein" = "online bartenders."

Of all the structural forms in classical music, however, none has proven more useful than the one known as sonata form. (The term "sonata" can be ambiguous, because it also refers to a work for a solo instrument. However, once Haydn began playing with the ways to compose string quartets and symphonies, sonata form was established.) It is one of the greatest achievements in Western art. That may sound hyperbolic, but it is not. It is safe to say that the first movement of every symphony, concerto, string quartet, and piano sonata in the classical canon uses this form. What is it, and why did it overwhelm all the other possibilities composers had at their disposal?

The basic idea of a sonata form, like that of Western music itself, is simple. Two contrasting themes are played, one after the other. (They are linked by a short transitional figure.) The important thing is that they are of an obviously differing character. In order to posit this information in the listener's memory, this opening section is played twice without variation. What follows is a section in which the two opposing themes are "developed." That means their intervals and rhythms are transformed and we the listeners get to explore some of the implications of those two tunes. In some cases, they seem to morph into each other. Once this section has come to an end, the magic happens: the two themes are brought back again in a recapitulation. We hear the themes in a new way. They are no longer opposites but part of a whole. The one does not exist without the other, and their external differences melt into a consistent whole. It is as if Papa Haydn and centuries of Western musicians all studied Chinese philosophy, in which two opposites are part of oneness.

To help show this oneness, the two themes heard in the first section are originally presented in different (but related) keys, but when they come back in the last section, they are played in the same key. Exposition (repeated)–development–recapitulation. That's it. Every first movement of every Beethoven symphony. Your favorite concerto. A Mozart string quartet you are hearing for the first time. And yet. . . .

I was attracted to classical music from a very early age and had absolutely no idea about structure. I just liked it. How did I manage to love this music without that knowledge? And I suspect many of you reading this might be asking the same question.

If there is one aspect of the power of music you do understand however, it is the power of memory and the joy of recapitulation. The finale of Sibelius's Symphony no. 2 contains just such a moment. A long transition out of the third movement sets up a tremendous sense of expectation when a glorious melody is stated, complete with triumphal fanfares. It then goes away. The composer gives us a break from it in a series of far less important sequences, until more than six minutes later that melody returns, leading to a great hymn of thanksgiving and joy. A big, beautiful melody is of course a great thing, and not easy to compose. But when, after a long time, the big melody returns, we are fulfilled.

The sonata movement created the template for the rewards of memory. Memory structures are, for example, how long jokes and witticisms work. Set up a humorous situation, continue speaking, and then refer back to it. Your brain connects the two and you laugh. Entire situation comedies on television make use of this technique, as do comedic plays. It activates your participation in the game: you are in on it and it rewards you.

The invention of the so-called potpourri overture in grand opera is another way a composer of an opera could make use of memory to create coherence. Before the curtain rises, you hear melodies that will be heard during the opera that has yet to be performed. It is like the hand you are being dealt at the start of a card game. (It is not surprising that Stravinsky loved playing card games.) Certain operas, like Mozart's *Le nozze di Figaro,* do not begin with a potpourri overture. However, in his *Don Giovanni* overture, Mozart predicts the music of the last scene, when the ghost of the man whom Giovanni murders in the first scene returns from the grave. The brain connects these two pillars, three hours later, and the effect is electrifying.

And understanding that—the power of memory—brings us to the genius of Richard Wagner and how he tapped into something that is even more basic and simple than all the structures created in the post-baroque eras. While those structures helped build a grand legacy of instrumental music,

Wagner ignored all of that (unlike his contemporary Brahms) and went back to the source of perceived structure in music— memory. It is not, therefore surprising that Brahms wrote in just about every classical medium except opera, and Wagner wrote only operas, which are, after all, overt musical stories.

Beauty and a seemingly inevitable and coherent process are the elements of our pleasure with classical music. And coherence can only exist with memory. In Wagner's first successful opera, *Rienzi,* he experimented with establishing continuity in an enormously long opera by constructing a thirteen-minute overture based on the various melodies from its five acts. Experiencing the opera, the audience is never more than fifteen minutes or so away from one of the great melodies presented in the famous overture—right to the last act, with Rienzi's prayer. The overture prepares the audience, acting like a series of introductions, so that when an aria or chorus emerges within the dramatic framework, there is recognition of something familiar. The mind harks back and has a eureka moment.

By the time Wagner came to the unprecedented idea of composing his *Ring* Cycle, and having composed the epic poem that constitutes its libretto, he had to solve the problem of how to keep some sense of continuity in telling the tale through four sequential operas, experienced over four days. What would hold the entire thing together? It certainly would not be by creating a potpourri overture before the first opera, or constructing a mammoth fifteen-hour sonata, a series of rondos, or themes and variations. (This was something that had to wait until the twentieth century with the two operas of Alban Berg, *Wozzeck* and *Lulu.* It is doubtful that anyone but those of us who have conducted these works can hear that each major character in *Lulu*, for example, is presented as structure:

all three scenes between Lulu and Dr. Schön are an embedded sonata, and so forth.)

What Wagner did was create a set of short musical motifs that are presented at important moments in the drama and seem to represent those moments, characters, objects, and emotions. The brain links the melody with a visually and dramatically memorable moment. This procedure mysteriously creates a permanent relationship between the music and the object. From that moment onward, each time the melody is heard in the unfolding drama brings us back to its first iteration, and since the *Ring* takes place over generations, the sense of time and nostalgia become ever more emotive.

When the body of Siegfried is carried from the Rhine riverbank to the Hall of the Gibichungs in the last opera, *Götterdämmerung*, we hear melodies that take us back to his parents, whom we last saw two operas ago; to Siegfried's fearless and virginal youth; to his heroic adulthood and his union with the goddess-turned-woman Brünhilde; and to the tragic now of the moment. In addition, Wagner, whose motifs for villains (the Giants, the Nibelungs, Hunding, and the rest) are almost exclusively rhythmic and not melodic, saves the simplest motif for the man who kills Siegfried: Hagen. His motif is two simple, repeated notes: "Ha-gen." In poetry, this would be called a spondee. The funeral music begins with these two violent stabs: Ha-gen! As the music proceeds, reminding us of all we have experienced in the story so far, we arrive at the point where Wotan's brilliant but flawed idea—to create an all-powerful sword that would be used to maintain the old order and his power—is magisterially summoned as it was first heard in the last moments of the first opera in the cycle, *Das Rheingold*, on a solo trumpet. Suddenly, those two stabbing accompanying notes are transformed through harmony

and orchestration from the sinister "Hagen" into the brilliant
"Siegfried"—a name that has the same simple two syllables:
Sieg-fried! The yin and yang, the dark and the light, the evil
and the good, are morphed before our ears! We remember
a story that began before the dead hero's parents were con-
ceived. We remember how we heard it for the first time at least
three nights before in whatever series of performances we are
attending. It is the monumental return on our investment of
time, the culmination of music and memory that marks Wagner as the genius he was.

One musicologist, Alfred Lorenz, attempted in the 1920s
to apply various structural matrixes onto the four operas of
The Ring, as if it were some grandiose four-movement symphony. It reads as being fairly ridiculous, if inventive, though
for many years his work was taken quite seriously as a way of
proving the value of Wagner's unique masterpiece.

A number of twentieth-century composers, including
Debussy and Stravinsky, revolted against Wagner's use of
musical motives linked to characters, objects, and emotions.
Debussy referred to this technique as giving each character a *carte de visite*. Wagner, it should be said, never wanted
names put on his themes of memory, and bristled at the word
"leitmotif" as well as any explicit definition of them. Nevertheless, in 1878, one of his employees at Bayreuth, Hans von
Wolzogen, did that very thing by publishing a list of motifs
from *The Ring* and giving them names, and it is not unusual
to read about the "Fate motif" or the "Redemption motif."
Wagner clearly had very specific associative ideas, but he was
concerned that they would be simplified and even vilified (as
they were by Debussy) if made explicit.

However, Wagner may have had the last laugh. When
Debussy composed his one completed opera, *Pelléas et*

Mélisande, he wanted to create something that felt like another Wagnerian romantic fantasy of medieval forbidden love, but not use motifs specifically associated with any character or situation. He also did not want the opera to be specific in its dramatic music. He began composing it in the middle, with the act-four love duet; and once he created a musical setting that was not a long passionate crescendo of emotions, he felt he had succeeded in something original and anti-Wagnerian.

The gloriously inventive score to *Pelléas,* universally praised today, has nonetheless failed to find its way into the central core, even though it is performed relatively often in large opera houses. It remains ultimately unsatisfying, mysteriously evading our comprehension. Is it descriptive? Yes. Is it evocative? Yes? Is it endlessly beautiful? Absolutely. Does it make you want to stay until the final curtain? Perhaps.

The first time I experienced *Pelléas* was as a twenty-year-old student in Paris, in 1966. The production was by a man who was at the center of twentieth-century French culture, the late writer, filmmaker, and artist Jean Cocteau, and took place at the Opéra-Comique, where *Pelléas* had received its world premiere in 1902. In other words, this would be historic from the points of view of both design and venue. After each act, I was able to improve where I sat until the end, when, I noted in my diary, there were more people in the orchestra pit and onstage than were in the house. I think I know why.

Debussy was intent on not pandering to the desires of the audience—i.e., the coherence of a closed form based on associations and recapitulation. There are no clearly perceived themes for the two main characters or their forbidden love. Some musicologists have attempted to find them, but also point out that these themes are constantly changing. Others say that the motifs are not associated with characters and objects but with feelings. All agree that they are rarely repeated without significant modifications in harmony and melodic outline. They might, therefore, account for how Debussy composed the opera, but not for how we might hear and understand it. Since the play upon which it is based is a symbolist play, you could argue that this was precisely the composer's point. Like the two characters in the first scene who encounter each other in a dark forest, we, too, are lost.

When we see Mélisande on her deathbed, there would have been an opportunity to bring back the music heard in the four previous acts; but no, Debussy gives us new material at a time when we have already reached sensory overload. If you compare this scene with the deathbed scene of Mimì in *La Bohème*, you will know what I mean. Melodies of Mimì's first encounter with Rodolfo take the audience back to that fateful and happy Christmas Eve and all that has transpired since. A tremendous wave of emotion engulfs us at her death because of remembrance of time past. Debussy wanted his story to keep on going. Mélisande's newborn daughter must now live onward toward an ambiguous future. While Debussy's dramatic solution is intellectually brave, it is not emotionally satisfactory—and was not intended to be. For those of us who love this unique opera, there is not much we can do except love what we love.

Although Debussy and Stravinsky rejected Wagnerianism, the Wagnerian technique perfected in his *Ring* Cycle was carried on in the operas of Richard Strauss and Alban Berg and the dramatic music of a generation of young men who studied in the German conservatories in the first quarter of the twentieth century. Without exception, they carried on this operatic tradition in their music for dramatic films when they became refugees from the Third Reich. You can see and feel how this works in hundreds of scores, such as Max Steiner's *Gone with the Wind* and Franz Waxman's *Sunset Blvd.*

As new generations of composers, mostly trained in American conservatories, took the reins of film composition, Wagnerian procedures were taken for granted as the method any composer uses to tell a cinematic story—what Erich Wolfgang Korngold referred to as "operas without singing." Motifs composed by John Williams for the first *Star Wars* film that represent certain characters and objects continue to hold the ever-expanding modern epic together over the lifetime of its audience members. In that way, Williams has done Wagner one better.

The German composer's score took decades to compose but was only revealed in its entirety in August of 1876. Wagner had hoped to present the entire cycle in one glorious world premiere, but his patron, King Ludwig II of Bavaria, became impatient and the first two operas received separate premieres—*Das Rheingold* in 1869 and *Die Walküre* in 1870. The world had to wait another six years to experience the complete work. In Williams's case (and in those of the composers who have continued using his motifs while adding new ones), the initial exposition of his score was in 1977. Well into the next century, new scores were emerging based on the originating motifs, making the saga a very personal one for millions of people who exhibit a constant state of expectation for new iterations of this basic compositional material. For millions of people, it is a foundational element in the soundtrack of their lives.

If the fundamental structural procedure of classical music is the use of memory, the question then arises as to whether there are pre-existing and generally accepted musical elements that composers employ to indicate meaning—musical memes that have developed over the centuries that we all remember from other musical works. Do we all have a collective musical dictionary of Western musical gestures, instrumental colors, and keys, whether or not we have studied music history? In other words, is all classical music "about" something, or is it abstract? When Stravinsky wrote that composers merely "combine notes," did he really mean that, and only that? Even in his middle and later years, he named his ballet scores after Greek culture, *Orpheus, Apollo,* and the Greek word for game, *Agon.*

There are many music philosophers who are adamant that music is not about anything, and that when it purports to be, it is of lesser value. In an 1875 letter to Brahms, Wagner admitted that his music has been accused of being merely "scenery" rather than music, because of his attempt to describe water, fire, clouds, and a rainbow.

The idea that music of value is free of associations, whether intended by the composer or inappropriately added by the listener, is a relic of a battle that was waged in the waning years of the nineteenth century and kept on life support through much of the twentieth by its avant-garde and others who wrote about and taught music. On the other hand, people have been describing their feelings upon listening to music for centuries. Even the most modern of postmodern composers continue to use musical gestures that "mean" something, whether it is the 2014 Pulitzer Prize–winning John Luther Adams, whose winning score has a clearly pictorial title, *Become Ocean,* or George Benjamin, whose 2018 opera, *Lessons in Love and Violence,* contains a scene in which the murder of a man is accompanied by music of "gnashing rage," as one critic described it. Clearly music is about something to many composers, too.

However music within the classical music canon may or

may not be telling a story per se, it is seemingly always refer-
ential to other works and gestures. As we progress from 1720
to the mid-twentieth century, the additive nature of music's
lexicon made it more and more possible to describe things and
feelings, even something as complex as "pretend fear," which
can be heard in scores to mash-up horror/comedy films like
Hold That Ghost (1941) and *Abbott and Costello Meet Frankenstein* (1948). Hans Salter and Frank Skinner's orchestral scores
trigger the audience's fear factor by their control of harmony
and orchestration, occasionally scaring you and sometimes
making you laugh at the absurdity of the various situations.
The intended audience for these films was not the intellectual
elite.

Every work within the classical canon sets up an overall
sound environment. Within its universe there is progression
toward something, even if that something feels like it is merely
its final cutoff. The composer has built this invisible structure
for you to hear. It could be a four-movement symphony, with
a sonata as its first movement, a gentle and nostalgic andante
second movement, a jocular series of courtly dances as a third,
and a monumentally triumphal finale. It could be a relatively
static oasis or a blaringly complex series of highly structured
orchestral densities. At the moment of its conclusion, in that
split second of silence, your brain does an instant recap of the
performance and, ideally, understands it.

Mozart's narrative and temporal world is hugely varied
but draws from a smaller dictionary of gestures—harmonies,
orchestral colors, time spans—than does Wagner's. That may
determine how much you prefer one composer to another. If
the composer has given you a title, you will inevitably use that
information to make overt sense of the work. If not, there are
many ways for you to enjoy its procession through time, and
we shall discuss them in due course.

When you have just been to a new play, someone might ask you "What was it about?" With classical music, that question cannot be answered. The question could be "What did it sound like?" You, however, will have felt something, experienced something, and may not have words to describe the experience, because it was visceral, emotional, or perhaps spiritual. And anyway, how does one describe something that is invisible and experiential? What it sounded *like* is a description of its surface or its style, and not its idea or its effect.

Part of the reason Western music has become the world's idea of classical music is its implied narrative/descriptive component. Humans love stories. Western classical music is a language of ambiguous but memorable nouns, operated upon by generally understood adjectives, adverbs, and dependent clauses, as well as completely comprehensible verbs that move it forward in perceived time. You, the auditor, are invited to supply the meaning for the nouns and thus tell your own story. That inspires the interaction, and interaction creates reality. You become the co-composer as well as the co-performer with us performers, collectively telling a wordless and personal tale.

· CHAPTER 6 ·

Pay Attention!

Leonard Bernstein's first televised appearance, on *Omnibus*,
November 15, 1954

MANY PEOPLE ENCOUNTER classical music as background music playing softly in waiting rooms at dentists' offices. Others play it quietly as they knit or read books on classical music. In New York City, calling 311 for nonemergency issues to kvetch about problems in their neighborhoods usually means waiting on hold for a number of minutes. That's when New Yorkers are likely to hear Mozart's Flute Concerto in G Major. There's a good reason why, as we shall see.

Does classical music need your full attention and must it exist in a separate physical place, a kind of nondenominational church? When Béla Bartók came to live in New York City in the last years of his life, he complained that there was just too much music everywhere. That was in the 1940s. For him, proper respect for music demanded that it exist in a dedicated environment—a place you went to; it shouldn't be something that invaded your everyday activities, like buying socks in a department store.

The way we listen to music exists on a spectrum from passive to active. Music exists in a sonic world of emotion and intellect. How we participate in it will vary from person to person according to our need to have music in our lives, especially now that music is everywhere to be heard and easily accessed. There is a limit to what neuroscientist Lisa Feldman Barrett calls your "body budget" and how much of your perception can address the sensory input from music. You are always navigating other aspects of your life while you are in the presence of it, and that will affect your ability to hear it in a multitude of ways. Music can legitimately be background, middle ground, or foreground. In each case, classical music justifies its existence, even when you take a nap in its presence—and you wouldn't be the first to do so.

The half-sleep state—something Wagner represented in his librettos (Elsa, Wotan, Siegmund, Hagen)—can be like sitting in your unconscious, free of all worldly cares and constraints. Surely the opening E-flat-major chord that starts *Das Rheingold* and lasts for five minutes was intended to set up the immense time scale of the storytelling, but was also meant to put the audience into that mysterious "story time" state when parents and grandparents read to us as children. Wagner based his *Ring* story on many sources, one of which is the collection of Icelandic myths known as the *Poetic Edda, edda* being a word that scholars in the nineteenth century believed to mean "great-grandmother."

Must there be silence in the room? If you are actively listening to classical music, the answer is yes, but it is important to remember that Telemann, Hindemith, and Mozart, among others, composed music for events like dinner parties and student revelries. That would not be true for a Mass or a symphony. We do know, however, that the wealthy frequently "visited" performances, since they owned their boxes at the opera house, and it was perfectly normal to come late, leave early, or spend a good deal of time staring at people in the hall. Before the use of electric light, and its innovative use by Wagner (again!), opera houses and concert halls were kept at the same lighting before, during, and after the performance. This makes perfect sense in the pre-gaslight era. Focusing on the stage was achieved in 1876 in Wagner's Festspielhaus in Bayreuth, where lights were dimmed during the performance and where there are no horseshoe-shaped balconies, as in traditional opera houses. If you think about it, that is why the side boxes in the oldest opera houses have limited views of the stage but unlimited views of other people in the audience.

A lot of citizen arrests are made in concerts when there is applause after a movement of a symphony because the people who are shushing firmly believe that in order to comprehend the totality of a symphony everyone should go from start to finish without the interaction—interruption—of the audience. Newspaper reports and letters by artists from the eighteenth and nineteenth centuries about world premieres and major concerts indicate frequent audience applause and demands for repeats of entire movements within symphonies. The joyful conclusion of the first movement of Beethoven's Symphony no. 2 asks for applause, and when there is none, it feels more like a rejection of the music than respect for its integrity. Stifling the natural response to classical music feels simply unnatural. It also leads many people to fear improper behavior and public humiliation, discouraging them from attending a classical concert by somehow indicating ignorance of strict protocol.

On June 21, 2017, violinist Sandy Cameron, the Czech National Symphony Orchestra, and I gave the world premiere of Danny Elfman's Violin Concerto. The four-movement work, which lasts over forty minutes, received prolonged applause after each movement. (Three of its four movements end quietly, it should be said.) We onstage could feel the active participation of the audience in hearing this work for the first time and with no preparation from recordings to give them a clue as to what note would follow what note, and how long each of the movements would be. It was heartening to hear their applause and seemed absolutely natural. Once the concerto is better known, however, there may be controversy as to whether or not it is proper to applaud before it is over.

One of the effects of classical music is to create an environ-ment. In addition to all the previous explanations and descrip-tions of nature, structures, and narratives, there's something else going on in Western music, and perhaps all music. Music controls behavior. This was something known to civic and religious leaders, from Pythagoras and the Roman Catholic Church to the people who choose the music to assuage the anger of citizens waiting to complain about the sanitation department. It can be a source of calm, of beauty, and of civility.

In a letter to the inspectors of the Conservatoire in Paris dated October 17, 1797, Napoleon wrote, "Among all the fine arts music is the one that exercises the greatest influence upon the passions, and is the one that the legislator should most encourage. A musical composition created by a master makes an unfailing appeal to the feelings and exerts a far greater influence than a good book on morals, which convinces one's reason but not one's habits." Napoleon also used music to welcome him when he marched into a new city and sent emis-saries ahead of time to commission and judge new works by local composers and thus link the populace with his invad-ing/liberating army. Attention was definitely being paid, and being paid for.

That, inevitably, begs the question of whether classical music is a force for good. Is it essentially salutary? In Glasgow, a colleague of mine at the Scottish Opera once said in response to a question I had about Mozart's opera *La clemenza di Tito*, "Just think 'civilization.'" Artists and artists' supporters like to make the case of the fundamental importance of the arts as a positive force for society, and of course it can be. However, one has to ask questions about what the arts can and cannot achieve. In classical music, the sense of the goodness of classi-cal music—a kind of conversion therapy for the unwashed—is basic to the grant application and outreach programs of many symphony orchestras. Indeed, there are numerous examples of how classical music makes our babies smarter and keeps crime down in London tube stations.

Music may be morally neutral, but is Western classical music morally neutral? Can it make us better, both individually as well as collectively? I believe it can, in the sense of bringing people with diverse political opinions and economic situations together *while they are under its influence*. Sports events bifurcate the audience and can occasionally lead to violence. When the music stops, the question should be asked: Are we better as a people? And "better" might also be a word worth considering, since my better is not necessarily your better.

One thing people can agree on is that music can and does affect behavior. It can lead people into a frenzy of violence. It can make illegal behavior seem acceptable. It can get us running on a treadmill. It is a powerful medium of social control that is inherently neither good nor bad. If military marches encourage young men into battle, making them feel proud as well as invincible, that might be good for one side but not the other.

Police were occasionally on call at the premieres of Verdi's operas because of expected public unrest engendered by the potent combination of political ideas with grand music, as was also the case in 1937 when the federal government of the United States attempted to shut down the premiere of Marc Blitzstein's opera *The Cradle Will Rock* in New York City. If you were against the unification of Italy, thought that the aristocracy had every right to rule, thought that unionism was dangerous to American business—or simply thought any political unrest was a bad thing—you might not have supported the concept that classical music was a force for good.

When classical music is used to celebrate things you do

not agree with—like playing Siegfried's funeral music from
1876 at Nazi rituals for their fallen generals in 1943—does
that affect the music, its composer, and your attitude toward
it now? When you attend a performance of *Carmina Burana*,
does it matter to you that those same Nazis used Carl Orff's
cantata as proof that Germany's living composers were still
writing masterpieces and that the work was used as a calling
card for the cultural legitimacy of the Third Reich? Leonard
Bernstein, for example, was particularly outraged when he
was accused of stealing from it in his 1971 score to *Mass*, since
he viewed it as "Nazi music."

Many non-Christians listen to the music commissioned by
the Church and love it. Recent musicology has suggested that
since Bach was a conservative Lutheran, he would have been
anti-Catholic, anti-Jewish, and anti-Muslim. Like Wagner in
the nineteenth century and Schoenberg in the twentieth, Bach
would have felt that German music was the greatest music of
all time and a fundamental aspect of the superiority of German culture.

So how do we square all these conflicting things? It certainly
has to do with how we co-construct the narratives inherent in
Western music. As I said earlier, the nouns in musical sentences are ambiguous, but the process is not. With or without
being a conservative Lutheran, you can still feel the hope and
secure optimism of intentionally religious works of a composer who holds differing views, just as you can appreciate the
aesthetic values of religious paintings and the paraphernalia of
ritual from many belief systems. As noted earlier, Handel was
Bach's exact contemporary and composed for the commercial
theater (opera) while Bach spent most of his life composing
for a church in Leipzig. Handel never married and was rich.
Bach rather famously fathered twenty and complained about

how underpaid he was. Does any of that matter? How we hear and value their music is a personal choice. What we exclude from our appreciation of their music is as important as what we include. We are always susceptible to casting composers and their works in our own image. That is what makes music so difficult to pin down while simultaneously touching on its extraordinary power.

When I was young, Verdi's Requiem was still being criticized for being too operatic for true church music—an astonishing criticism of its appropriateness from the gold and glitter of the Roman Catholic Church. One of the essential aspects of Verdi's masterpiece is not its operatic setting of the text to a Catholic Mass, but its ambiguity *toward* the Catholic Church itself. The conclusion of this Requiem is the most human of outcries, whose final demand God never answers: "Libera me"—Deliver me. This is the opposite of another iconic religious work, the "Hallelujah" Chorus. In its own way, Verdi's Requiem captures the crisis of faith and what that loss of security means in our lives. Handel's *Messiah* reaffirms it. Once again, classical music opens itself to us no matter who we are and what we believe. It invites us all in, even when it is dressed as a Catholic Mass for the dead or an English oratorio by a German composer that attempts to demonstrate that Jesus is the Messiah by musicalizing predictive passages from the Old Testament and ending with Christ's glorification in heaven.

Does Western classical music civilize or proselytize? Loving certain types of music creates a sense of community, a club in which we feel acceptance. When classical music creates an environment of anti-antisocial behavior, we see it as a force of good, unless we want social change through anarchic behavior. Then classical music becomes another opiate of the masses.

Here's why I do think classical music is ultimately a force of good, even if its composers were not the kind of people with whom you want to have dinner, or if the political exigencies of the time are not congruent with your own political point of view. In one of his greatest lectures, Leonard Bernstein concluded his 1954 television debut speaking about Beethoven, whom he considered to be the greatest composer of all time. I believe we can expand what he said to all classical music. It boils down to what Bernstein called "inevitability." Embracing all we have said so far regarding nature, time manipulation, and structures built from invisible yet palpable things, classical music exudes a sense of certainty that is greater than Benjamin Franklin's famous "death and taxes." And for some inexplicable reason, composers and their translators—we musicians—dedicate our lives to this principle.

Bernstein was in awe of Beethoven for "[giving] away his life and his energies just to make sure that one note follows another with complete inevitability." And here is Bernstein's great conclusion: "[Beethoven] leaves us at the finish with the feeling that something is right in this world . . . something that follows its own law consistently, something we can trust and that will never let us down."

And there you have it. Classical music in the central canon will never let you down. Each of the composers whose music we choose to hold dear persuades us that his logic is ours. All of this confronts what many scientists believe about the processes of our universe. In his book *The Order of Time,* theoretical physicist Carlo Rovelli explains that moving from order to disorder is more probable than the reverse. Within the idea of the Big Bang there is the implication that the universe in previous millennia—beginning 18.8 billion years ago—was in a state of high order that is constantly moving toward chaos.

This evolution results in the concepts of process and time. Putting humanity in the context of this scenario is daunting. Humans first appeared a mere 200,000 years ago on a very insignificant planet currently surrounded by 10^{22} stars.

Classical music confronts our numerical insignificance and the inevitable chaos that surrounds us and presents a counterproposal—an argument that inspired Einstein to find a proof that everything in the universe works like Mozart, balanced, beautiful, and interconnected. For us nonphysicists, observing the natural world, politics, human suffering, and our own aging process make an impressive case for Rovelli's theory. It is, however, a theory. And even if we are fooling ourselves, classical music creates a parallel universe, one that both feels immutable and is kept dazzlingly alive through its constant reinterpretation by living performers.

It also projects optimism. No matter how circuitous the journey, the vast majority of works in the standard repertory end in joy, and many in triumph. People sometimes make fun of the "fake Hollywood ending," but classical music has been insisting on happily-ever-after for centuries. There are so few works that end in tragedy, alienation, or unredeemed horror—until classical music enters the twentieth century—that we can look at this phenomenon as part of what makes classical music so beloved. It is the hoped-for ending we desire. Even at its most turbulent—Beethoven comes to mind—the music insists, and sometimes thunderously so, that all will be well. There is an entire subgenre of operas called "rescue operas"—its meaning should be pretty obvious—of which Beethoven's *Fidelio* is a prime example.

The fundamental residue of the Greek modes is that people hear music in a major key as happy and in a minor key as sad or tragic. We are all truly sensitive to the subtle distinction that depends on a small adjustment of the middle note in a three-note chord that turns a major chord into a minor one, whether you even know what a chord is. All nine of Beethoven's symphonies end in a major key. When the Berlin Philharmonic and Claudio Abbado programmed their New Year's Eve concert in 1999, celebrating the end of a millennium, every work on the program ended in a happy major key: A major from Beethoven and Stravinsky, G major from Dvořák, D major from Mahler, B-flat major from Prokofiev, and a final, resounding C major from Arnold Schoenberg's "Dawn" from his early cantata *Gurrelieder*. In celebrating a period that presumably focused on the politically and artistically turbulent twentieth century—and that, as it was also a millennial event, could have included the entire history of classical music—all its stories ended in uplift in Berlin as it exited the twentieth century.

It is not as if classical music is foolishly and naively happy. It always earns its conclusions, and listeners would do well to pay attention to the process that achieves them. And when those conclusions are tragic, like the finale to Tchaikovsky's Symphony no. 6, the *Pathétique*, or Schubert's song cycle *Winterreise* (Winter Journey), we should take note of the exception and embrace their legitimacy. We shall discuss romantic opera later on, since, unlike chamber music and symphonic works, romantic operas do in fact frequently end in tragedy—and with a minor chord at the final curtain. (Most German romantic operas in the standard repertory, however, do not.)

All of the above has very little to do with studying music at a conservatory. It can all be understood simply by paying attention right from the start. Most people would never begin reading a book at chapter 2, or come in late for a movie—especially one you have never seen before. Composers of

classical music write so as to lead you from its top to its conclusion. Sometimes, they will simply drop you into a work,
like Glinka's overture to *Ruslan and Ludmila*. Before you have
taken a breath, you are on a five-and-a-half-minute toboggan
ride. Sometimes (more often than not) a composer of long
works starts with a slow introduction. Pay attention! This
material may return or may simply pull you into the unique
universe of your journey.

Beethoven's nine symphonies are an easy way to experience both concepts—provided you are ready at the start. His
Symphony no. 8 is like Glinka's overture: we are thrust into
its exposition at the very first bar with no introduction what-
soever. However, in his Symphony no. 2, the introduction is
of an unprecedented length for its time (1802), lasting three
minutes and taking up 30 percent of the duration of the first
movement. And to give you some idea of the surprises that
await, whereas the first movement of his Second Symphony
ends with an almost finalelike conclusion, the end of the first
movement of the Eighth ends with a merry prank: a quiet
snippet of the big tune that started the movement so brilliantly
ten minutes before.

Beethoven is never one to be predicted, even though, as
Bernstein pointed out, once you are under his spell, everything appears to be inevitable. Today, it is hard to imagine the
shock of the opening of his Fifth Symphony, which, like the
Eighth, grabs you by the collar and pulls you in. Then, imagine being a curious Viennese attending the premiere of his
Symphony no. 9. (Perhaps you can recall when you first heard
it; if you haven't yet heard it, you have my envy at the discovery that awaits you.) Could you ever have predicted the opening of its immense first movement, or predicted its size and
shape? That said, once Beethoven has beckoned you to enter

its cosmic universe, you will be transformed into a consenting tourist of time and space, looking up at the stars and simultaneously down on earth, embracing the family of humanity. Beethoven achieved this more than a century before the world saw photographic images of our little blue-green planet floating in a sea of black and white. Classical composers are full of ideas and their genius is in their ability to share them with you.

If you are paying attention, you will experience another way of composing when you listen to Tchaikovsky's "overture fantasy" *Romeo and Juliet*. By its title and generic description you know two things: its subject matter and that the work is a fantasy of some kind. But what kind? Usually an overture is just that: an opening for something that follows it, perhaps an opera or a ballet. Instead, here it is a stand-alone work. Even before a single note is heard, Tchaikovsky has perhaps made you wonder how he will deal with the subject matter of Shakespeare's play.

It begins with a rather Russian-sounding church hymn. If you are engaged beyond letting it wash over you, it might occur to you that this music is a depiction of Friar Lawrence. For over four minutes we are in this sepulchral music, imbued with sadness and religiosity. Then there is a transition that gets us into violent music that seems to describe a fight. Montagues and Capulets, you conclude. Another transition deftly takes us to music that can only be love music: the ecstatic beauty of two naive and star-crossed teenagers. The composer then leads us back to the conflict, bigger and more violent than before. This time the religious music is played on the brass, as if fighting the battle music: the church vs. hatred. The love theme returns in a full and passionate repeat of its first iteration and then defiantly confronts the battle music, with the church music joining in. The violence wins, and over a long-sustained note on the tuba with a dirgelike rhythm from the timpani, the music expresses heartbreak as the love theme decomposes before us. The organlike chords from the opening return with profound meaning for us, because we have seemingly experienced a lifetime in twenty-two minutes. Over a keening bass line, the love theme cries out. A timpani roll and slashing chords bring the fantasy to an end.

Was that a story? Yes. Was it linear? No. That is, unless you conclude (the thinking and analyzing part of your brain) that it might be linear: the music starts by taking us back to "story time," and we see Friar Lawrence before the dead bodies of these two beautiful young people, and he thinks back to the conditions that brought him (and us) to this place. The concluding music, therefore, returns us to a few moments after Friar Lawrence began his remembrance and sadness—twenty-two minutes of durational time, but a few seconds in his thought process. Clearly, you could choreograph it that way. But it works as a concert piece because it plays in the theater of your mind, which, like your dreams, does not require a linear narrative.

In Debussy's early tone poem *Prelude to the Afternoon of a Faun*, he does something equally unexpected right at the start. He announces a theme on an unaccompanied flute. If you are hearing this work in a concert, there will be eighty-five musicians sitting there and one person playing, all alone. Pay attention to this melody, because each time it comes back it will be wearing a different costume, accompanied by different harmonies and sung by a different group of instruments. In that sense it is extraordinarily simple, and yet it is also a tour de force of transformation. German composers would probably have developed this evocative melody by changing its notes and stretching its intervals, but not appreciably changing its orchestration. Debussy clearly believed that changing the colors of the melody is a legitimate reason to move forward in time and to justify the composition itself. Its final iteration, on muted horns and the first violins playing the harmony and not the melody, is a plangent farewell to a journey that juxtaposes stasis with subtle transformation.

Within the canon, Ravel's *Boléro* is the ultimate example of this concept. In all cases, development is determined by something that stays the same, so that you can measure what is changing. This is how classical music works if you choose to pay attention rather than let it wash over you in a pleasant and passive way.

As you read this you have little awareness of how fast you are physically traveling—something like a thousand miles an hour at the equator (slower as you move toward the poles). If one object in the room simply stopped right now, you would understand, because you could compare everything to that one stationary object. The same is true of classical music and how composers play with keeping something constant while changing other aspects of the music. It is not particularly difficult to join the game, and the rules are embedded in the very start of every work in the canon.

Our senses are all interconnected. Italians tend to use the verb *sentire* for all of them, whereas other languages separate them into hearing, seeing, feeling, smelling, and tasting. At one point in the libretto to Mozart's *Don Giovanni*, the title character says, "Mi pare sentir odor di femmina!" (I sense the fragrance of a woman!). Human mouths have only five or six kinds of taste perceptions: salty, sweet, bitter, sour, *umami* (savory), and perhaps fat. Our noses, however, can detect a trillion distinct aromas. How we perceive music is probably closer to what our noses can do, though it would be impossible to create the data pool for it, such is its complexity.

In March 2017 a short video went viral that showed a ten-year-old boy, Cayson Irlbeck, who was born color-blind, being given a pair of glasses that filtered out some aspect of light and allowed him for the first time to see color. Ironically, by limiting his sensory input to mimic what most "normal" people see, he was able to differentiate colors for the first time. His response—to turn to his father, sobbing with emotion—was something millions of people saw and felt the need to share. What was also important is that the boy was not blind. He was color deficient. When his senses were opened up by eliminating extraneous data, something profound happened to him and the way he will experience life forevermore.

That is what happens when people open themselves to classical music. It has filtered out the noise and thereby exposed that which was buried within. Yes, music has always been there, but classical music contains all those colors and density shifts that you might not have been aware of. The result is a new perception into life, and a joining with others who have collectively lived or imagined every experience—some of which you have never experienced or never admitted to. It is that Cayson Irlbeck moment, when Mozart, Debussy, and Wagner enter your life.

· CHAPTER 7 ·

The First Time: Weaving the Web of Continuity

Marie Antoinette's little theater at Versailles, where she performed
the role of Rosina in Beaumarchais's play *The Barber of Seville*,
before she was arrested and ultimately executed in 1793

I S THERE A WAY TO PREPARE for a first encounter with a piece of music? Is it by a composer you already know? Is it a composer you have heard about but whose music you have never heard? Is it a complete unknown in every sense of the word—and are you dreading it? All of these categories create new and unique opportunities. Let's take a look at them.

In 1810, the German composer/conductor/writer E. T. A. Hoffmann, the man who would create the modern fairy tale with his *Nutcracker and the Mouse King*, read the published score of Beethoven's latest symphony, the one simply called no. 5, and discovered something unexpected, life altering, and clearly a game changer for music. (He had not yet heard the symphony performed.) He wrote an enormously long review in a Leipzig publication that would have immense influence. Here's a segment:

> Beethoven's music . . . discloses to us the realm of the colossal and the immeasurable. Beams of incandescent light shoot through the deep night of this realm, and we become conscious of enormous shadows; shadows that, in the ponderous weight of their alternating ebb and flow, ever-more-narrowly constrain, and, ultimately, annihilate *us*—without, however, annihilating that pain of infinite yearning upon which each and every pleasure that has fleetingly come into its own in the exultation of melody founders and then perishes, and it is only in virtue of this pain—this pain of mingled love, hope, and joy that is intrinsically consumptive but not destruc-

tive, this pain that strives to tear our breast asunder in a full-voiced concord of all the passions—that we survive the ordeal as enraptured communicants with the great beyond!

One can only feel a certain envy at the discovery Hoffmann expresses here. Can that ever happen to you? The answer is yes.

In a real way, that is what millions of people were experiencing in the 1960s with the rediscovery of the symphonies of Gustav Mahler, now so normal in concert halls. You can never predict that moment, and most of us probably don't have the capacity to put our feelings into the words of a Hoffmann; but the experience of life-affirming recognition is always inherent in the potential energy of a work that is new to you—and, quite frankly, of a work you "know" when performed by a great translator. You may hear yourself say, "I never heard it like that before."

More important, your first time with a piece of music will inevitably be a *performance*, recorded or live. That means you will conflate the discovery of a work with its performance, and the two elements will inform all subsequent performances. "No one ever conducted Mahler like Bernstein" is still frequently heard decades after the maestro's death in 1990. Those performances and the discoveries that were made years ago created markers in people's memories and life experiences. A personal story was begun, a port of entry, one that will be held dear to each person for the rest of their lives.

On March 19, 1965, I attended a live performance of Puccini's *Tosca* at New York's Metropolitan Opera House. It was not a new production. *Tosca* was an opera I had only heard on studio recordings, and I owned three of them. I was nine-

teen years old and I knew my *Tosca*. There was a reason I
had worked so hard to acquire a ticket for that particular
night. Maria Callas was returning to the New York stage
after a seven-year absence and a history of cancellations and
an endless series of gossip-column inches in magazines and
newspapers. As hard as it may be to imagine that time in the
cultural history of classical music, there were people marching
outside the Met wearing placards reading, "Franco Corelli:
The World's Greatest Tenor." His fans did not want Callas to
overshadow him.

If you do not know *Tosca*, Puccini sets up her act 1 entrance
with a brilliant mixture of action (an escaped prisoner bursts
into an ornate Roman Catholic church) and romance (a tenor
sings an aria of his love for the title character). When she
arrives, it is her voice we first hear offstage. She sings the name
of her lover—"Mario!"—as she gets closer and closer, repeating his name.

That night, 3,849 people heard a voice I knew only from
recordings. I remember describing the feeling within the audience. It was as if someone near the edge of the orchestra pit
had put his finger in an electrical outlet and all of us, joined
together, felt a shock of 120 volts pass through our bodies as
we were instantaneously transformed from a group of opera
fans into a tribe. And when she entered, carrying an enormous
bouquet of yellow roses and in a costume designed for her by
Marcel Escoffier, we went mad. That is the only word for it,
and recordings of that moment are available for the curious:
two minutes of unforgettable hysteria.

Years have passed and there has been many another *Tosca*
in my life, some experienced as part of the audience and some
from the vantage point of the conductor's podium, but that
night at the Met is where my *Tosca* starts, acting retroactively

on those studio recordings and then setting an impossible and delicious standard from which all performances will forever be measured.

In a way, there was no preparing me for that experience, even though I knew a good deal about the work and its performers before I arrived at the old opera house. But there are things you *can* do, if you wish, to give yourself some parameters of expectation, some clues to go beyond naïve discovery. Some, it should be said, just want to be surprised by a new work. I do not.

If nothing else, I like to know how long a new work is going to be. That information usually can be found in program notes; and if you are listening to a recording, it is easily accessible. The reason for that is to allow your brain to get a general idea of the process you will experience within its durational time. It's like having a countdown clock while the work is moving forward. When you read a printed book, you always know where you are within it by measuring the distance that remains between its covers.

At the world premiere of Ravel's *Boléro* in 1928, it is said that a woman began to shout after fifteen minutes of its numbingly repeated melody—eighteen orchestrations of the same tune played over a repeated snare-drum rhythm—"Au fou! Au fou!" (He's mad! He's mad!). Had she known it would all be over a minute later, she might have reserved judgment. But how could she have known? It might have gone on for another seemingly interminable fifteen minutes.

Knowing when a piece of music was written (and where) is another easily found bit of information. As we discussed earlier, historical time will give you a point of reference. If you believe in the concept of modernism or that chronology is an important element in your admiration of a work, the date might be even more important. It was said that Liszt "invented the *Tristan* chord." That famous combination of intervals haunts Wagner's opera and became a musical reference point for decades whenever a composer wanted to telegraph death-haunted love. Liszt may have invented this chord, but Wagner wrote *Tristan*. Chronology is interesting, but hardly a reason to love or dismiss a piece of music.

Putting music into historical context, however, is another matter. It not only invites us to imagine its time but also creates the environment in which we can compare it with our own knowledge and our own time. Most classical music lovers know two plays by the French playwright, watchmaker, and spy Beaumarchais: *The Barber of Seville* and *The Marriage of Figaro*. Although the famous operas based on those plays were composed in reverse chronological order—Rossini's *Barber* was composed in 1813, and Mozart's *Figaro* in 1786—knowing what Beaumarchais was up to between the writing of his two plays (1775 and 1781) is enlightening: He worked for King Louis XVI to support the American Revolution as both a spy and an operative providing funds, munitions, and supplies to the colonists. In France, the successful American Revolution and the corruption of the monarchy led to more open hostility in Beaumarchais's depiction of the upper class in the second play, which was initially condemned by the censors. The young count in Rossini's opera (the hero) and the delightful woman he ultimately marries (the wily and brilliant Rosina) become the amoral count and his miserably unhappy wife in the second play, set to music by Mozart. The DNA of the politics of America, France, Spain, Italy, Austria, and England are all wrapped up in those beloved "standard repertory" operas. Marie Antoinette ultimately persuaded her husband to allow performances of *Figaro*. She enjoyed playing the role of Ro-

sina in *The Barber of Seville*, and acted it in her last performance at her private theater on August 19, 1785. (She was
arrested in June 1791 and beheaded on October 16, 1793.)

Americans can also find a certain ownership of the Mozart
opera, since the man who adapted Beaumarchais's play for its
musical setting, Lorenzo da Ponte, outlived Mozart by many
years and became the first professor of Italian literature at
Columbia University in New York City, dying as an American citizen in 1838.

And therein lies the point: A bit of history about a piece of
music we are hearing for the first time invites us to enter its
world by overlaying context onto its sounds.

Sometimes you will hear music by a composer who is well
known to you, perhaps even a favorite, but the work itself is
unfamiliar. This can be an early work, one that predates the
famous pieces that have entered the canon, and you will file it
as "juvenilia." Composers sometimes take time to find their
unique voices. Others seem to be born sounding like themselves. It took Mozart a bit of time, but Tchaikovsky and Bernstein seemed to have entered the compositional world sounding
the way we have come to expect them to sound right from the
start. (In fairness to Mozart, his first works were composed at
the age of five.) Beethoven just kept getting more and more
profound, even as his early works are sufficient unto themselves. Unfamiliarity, therefore, can present fascinating challenges and surprising opportunities for discovery, provided
the composers you know had significant support (financial
and moral) and sufficient health to develop and bloom during
their lifetime. Every note you ever heard by George Gershwin
was composed in an eighteen-year period, from 1919 (his first
hit song, "Swanee") until 1937, the year he died of a brain
tumor at the age of thirty-eight, making the opportunity for

his development as a composer quite short. Not so with Verdi, who lived into the twentieth century, dying at eighty-seven, or Richard Strauss, who lived from 1864 to 1949. Any work by either composer can be compared and contrasted with another you already know, and simply knowing how old they were and what was going on in the world—politically, artistically, and philosophically—will bring enlightenment and understanding not only to the new work but to the ones you already know. Some composers collapsed entirely, as Sibelius did in the 1920s, leaving us absolutely nothing from the last thirty years of his life.

Stravinsky, on the other hand, made a career out of "outliving [his] fame," as he once said, which he attempted by his lifelong quest to be ahead of the latest trends in twentieth-century modernism. It is unlikely that you will hear any of his 1910 *Firebird* in his 1966 *Requiem Canticles*. That said, you might take a work of Stravinsky you do know and listen to his next major work, tracing the composer's directionality and reaction to his own last composition. Is there, for example, any audible relationship between *The Rite of Spring* (1913) and *Song of the Nightingale* (1917)? You may find that while the style keeps changing, something consistent runs through all the works—or you may not. Part of the manifesto of the avant-garde was to destroy any sense of continuity of style in order to ensure vitality and modernity. Other composers do a sudden reboot, having reached a kind of impasse, establishing a new and consistent voice. This happened frequently in the first half of the twentieth century. You may find it difficult to square early Kurt Weill (his Violin Concerto and his expressionist opera *Der Protagonist)* with the composer of *The Threepenny Opera* and *Street Scene*. The same holds true of Prokofiev and Hindemith.

The violent and passionate Richard Strauss of *Salome* and *Elektra* would never have predicted the pastel and intellectual Richard Strauss of his last opera, *Capriccio*. However, if you listen to his 1909 *Elektra* and then follow it with his next opera, the 1911 *Der Rosenkavalier,* you might be surprised at how similar they are—something impossible to hear when you see these operas. In the opera house, the former will show you a filthy and decaying courtyard of an ancient Greek palace and the latter will take place in richly decorated Viennese rooms with singers costumed as if Mozart had composed the score. Of course there is a significant change in style in Strauss's attempt to re-create the violence inherent in Greek tragedy from 400 BC and a romanticized Vienna of the 1740s, with nineteenth-century-sounding Viennese waltzes applied to the latter. The waltz, it should be added, did not exist in Mozart's time, but like Verdi's imaginary evocation of ancient Egypt, no one minds hearing waltzes while seeing powdered wigs on the stage. Indeed, *Elektra* has its waltzes, too, but you may not hear them as such unless you close your eyes and listen. One of the advantages to hearing recordings of these operas is that the composer's similarities will be on display without the distraction of visualization.

I had never heard Rachmaninoff's Symphony no. 1 until 2017, which is when Vladimir Jurowski and the London Philharmonic Orchestra brought it to Lincoln Center. This symphony, composed in 1895, had a disastrous world premiere in St. Petersburg two years later. Its second performance had to wait until 1945, after the composer's death. For someone who has performed many of Rachmaninoff's works, the 2017 performance was a joyous experience of pattern matching. What proved overwhelming was the composer's frequent quotation from the medieval chant for the dead, known as Dies irae.

This same melody has haunted the Western canon for centuries (Mozart, Berlioz, and Verdi make use of it), but, more importantly, it is a frequent ingredient in Rachmaninoff's mature works, like his very last orchestral piece, the *Symphonic Dances,* composed on Long Island in 1940. I was therefore hearing his First Symphony in antichronological terms—from the vantage point of the end of his compositional life—and was taken by the fact that as a young man he was already fascinated with death and mortality. As I noted earlier, classical music plays with and confronts time.

The public is inexplicably finicky in what enters the general repertory, even when a composer is immensely popular. Why do we know certain Beethoven sonatas and not others? Is it a question of quality, or is it some ineffable aspect of its compositional materials and how they are manipulated by the composer? Why do we all know Gershwin's *Rhapsody in Blue* but not his *Second Rhapsody*? Indeed, Tchaikovsky is perhaps the most popular composer in the world. At the Hollywood Bowl, an all-Tchaikovsky program routinely generates over fifty thousand tickets sold on a three-concert weekend. No other classical composer could do that, not even Beethoven. However, although there is a lot of Tchaikovsky to hear and enjoy, the public has embraced only a relatively small percentage of his output: his last three symphonies (out of six), his Violin Concerto, one piano concerto (out of three), one overture-fantasy (out of three), a solemn overture which he thought was "loud and noisy," and all three of his ballet scores. In addition to a few other works (perhaps his opera *Eugene Onegin*) the fact is that Tchaikovsky's output includes eighty opus-numbered works—meaning they are considered major compositions. There are orchestral suites, string quartets, eleven operas, songs, piano pieces, and choral music.

There is, therefore, plenty of Tchaikovsky to hear for the first time if you are curious.

The experience will be enlightening. Perhaps you will find something you really love, like his one-movement Piano Concerto no. 3. Hearing one of his operas will give you a better understanding of the composer's intent when he is writing music without words. You may also understand why these works are not more often played, and that, too, will give you insight into the unpredictable nature of greatness, even from geniuses. It will make the works you love even more precious.

While I was working on a project that involved all of Tchaikovsky's lesser-known orchestral works, something occurred to me that I had never thought of before. A melody not only should be memorable, it should mysteriously exude a strange implication of its use. Is it a song? Will it become a concerto so that its contours can be the object of a give-and-take between soloist and orchestra? Is it worthy of a symphony? Tchaikovsky was particularly brilliant at figuring out the implication of his sketches and inventions. For example, his Piano Concerto no. 3 started out as a symphony, which was subsequently abandoned, most probably because the melodies neither could withstand the "pressure" of symphonic exposure nor implied the movements that would follow.

All of this might sound too esoteric for some, but if you listen to Tchaikovsky's four orchestral suites, you will hear what I mean. The music is pure Tchaikovsky, but the actual materials from which each movement is constructed could never support the high drama and long-form contrasts of his symphonies 4, 5, and 6. You will get an insight into the composer's dispassionate self-criticism. While he did not want to discard the melodies, he knew what they could and could not do.

For every Tchaikovsky and Rachmaninoff whose music

you easily encounter, there seem to be hundreds of composers from the last century whose music has disappeared from the concert halls and opera houses. You may find their names on a program and feel a certain trepidation toward hearing their music because you have been told that music disappears from being performed "for a reason," and that reason is, to put it bluntly, that the music is not good. You would do well to read about the underlying circumstances for their disappearance, since the twentieth century was a century of wars in which classical music was used as a weapon and a target.

Composers with names like Egon Wellesz, Mario Castelnuovo-Tedesco, and Walter Burle Marx are little known figures who composed during the closing years of the canon. Whenever you see a name of a composer from that period, it is worth taking a listen and keeping an open mind. In a world consumed with battles of cultural superiority and subsequent retaliation, suffering, and cleansing, composers and their music frequently became collateral damage. Remember the rediscovery and embrace of Mahler in the 1960s? It could happen to others, provided their music is played.

In 1988, I brought a recording of Erich Wolfgang Korngold's Symphony in F-sharp to Leonard Bernstein's country home in Fairfield, Connecticut. It was a rare event to have dinner with him and no one else. After dinner, I asked if he would be willing to hear something I had discovered and found particularly interesting.

I played the first movement of the symphony. Bernstein only knew that it was a symphony and therefore might have expected it to be in four movements. After intently listening to the twelve-minute movement, he had no idea who the composer was, but he liked the music enough to ask to hear the second movement. And so it went, after each movement I gave

him a chance to beg off. The symphony's third movement—
its emotional climax—inspired him to jump to the piano and
repeat its opening motif and the devastating substitution in its
harmonic structure that happens about twenty seconds into
it. After the last movement, I told him who had composed it.
I also told him that though the piece was completed in 1952,
its concert premiere did not take place until 1972, fifteen years
after the composer's death.

On first hearing, Bernstein thought the symphony should
have ended with the third movement, which would have
made it a very tragic symphony indeed. I suspect he heard
it in terms of late Mahler, which is appropriate enough. He
had not predicted—or perhaps wanted—its upbeat finale that
takes the gentle second theme of the first movement and transforms it into a positive march, albeit with a dark warning just
before its conclusion.

Be that as it may—classical music, even for Leonard
Bernstein, takes more than one hearing to reveal itself—
experiencing his "figuring it out" was both fascinating and
uplifting. Bernstein professed love for the music of Max
Steiner around that same period, and I am sure he would have
turned his attention to Korngold had he not passed away in
1990. Ironically, one of his mentors, Dimitri Mitropoulos, had
stated in 1959 that he had finally found "the perfect modern
work" and planned to perform the Korngold symphony the
next season with the New York Philharmonic, but his death
intervened.

Quite often a first hearing will be a brand-new piece by a
living composer. This can be the most exciting time for you,
hearing a voice from now and having a composer present in
the room, maybe even conducting the new work in front of
you. It can also be the most frustrating, especially if the work

is uncomfortably placed before or sandwiched in the middle of the standard works from another century. This makes demands on your brain that will usually lead to an inability to hear beyond the surface complexity of the new work. It will sound so different that it may feel as if it had landed from another planet.

Part of the reason is that this kind of programming, which has become typical in our time, makes the historical space between the new work and the standard ones greater every year. Without any kind of aesthetic link, our emotional and cognitive responses allow us little time to translate the input beyond generalized feelings. Many people come away from the experience with a simple question: Why?

Keeping an open mind is essential. Certain living composers are famous within the classical music world, and you may have heard other works by them. That, of course, makes your partnership with them a lot easier. Frequently composers' music can be heard on various Internet platforms, which will help get you into the general kind of music you will be hearing. Previews by enthusiastic journalists and in the written program notes may be helpful, or they may make matters even more confusing. Too much technical jargon will be off-putting, and contemporary writers continue to grapple with the nineteenth-century question of whether music is "about" anything other than the process of its notes—and so are some composers themselves.

Perhaps it is a normal human process to anthropomorphize all things: animals especially, but also plants and music, too. Watch people at an aquarium and they will say hello to a fish that is staring back from the other side of the tank. Perhaps a guide will tell you that the octopus clinging to the glass has both short-term and long-term memory capacity, that it is switched from one tank to another regularly so it doesn't get bored, and that games have been devised for the eight-legged creature to play. We learn that trees communicate with each other through various means, and elephants give out signals by the way they walk, all of which begs the question of whether we are being silly to imagine our fellow creatures as if they were human, or whether indeed all living creatures share the same traits and just express them in different ways. Since music is a human invention, it does relate to the communicative sounds of animals—dolphins, whales, finches, and all things big and small. It also makes sense that we have no choice but to process classical music in terms of our humanity.

You may read highly conflicted and conflicting descriptions of a new piece of music, and you should simply take this in stride. One of the many transitions we are going through right now is whether serious music critics permit themselves to break with the strongly held theory that music is simply music.

Before a world premiere in New York City in 2018, *The New York Times* published two preview articles about Anna Thorvaldsdottir's *Metacosmos*. In one of those articles, William Robin wrote: "Observers tend to link Ms. Thorvaldsdottir's willfully craggy music to the surreal tectonics of her native Iceland. But her expansive works defy such national clichés, and instead frequently channel abstract metaphysical concepts into acutely mysterious forms." That would seem to deny Icelandic imagery in her music. I won't attempt to decipher the second part of the sentence. "Mysterious," indeed.

The composer is also quoted as saying her work is "speculative metaphor of falling into a black hole." A speculative but not an actual metaphor: what does that mean? A metaphor that is considering the possibility of being a metaphor, perhaps?

Five days later, Joshua Barone described *Metacosmos* as taking on "the might and mystery of celestial bodies," which sounds descriptive enough, though not Icelandic.

Once you arrived at the concert, you might have read in the official program note that Alan Gilbert, the Philharmonic's former music director, who had chosen Ms. Thorvaldsdottir to win the orchestra's Kravis Emerging Composer Award, felt, in direct contradiction to the *Times,* that "her uncompromising approach to building soundscapes creates a visceral, pictorial aesthetic that is deeply connected to her Icelandic heritage." The note from the Philharmonic's program annotator, James M. Keller, contradicts the *Times* as well: "Thorvaldsdottir's music often suggests natural landscapes through sustained, sculptural sounds. She favors large-scale structures in which a wide variety of meticulously delineated timbres and sound combinations flow within a lyrical, sometimes enigmatic, atmosphere."

To add to the information a dutiful reader might seek out before a world premiere, the composer herself stated that "chaos versus beauty is built into the piece based on this power struggle idea." An indication in the score says, "When you see a long sustained pitch, think of it as a fragile flower that you need to carry in your hands and walk the distance of a thin rope without dropping it or falling."

This sounds a lot like actual metaphors and a few similes, too. Since the work has an interplanetary title, *Metacosmos,* which means something like "outside the universe," and shares a similar musical language with Ligeti's 1961 *Atmosphères,* which was used on the soundtrack to Stanley Kubrick's *2001: A Space Odyssey,* it all makes a kind of cinematic (i.e., narrative) sense. The one fact that everyone could agree on is the estimated performance duration published in the program: approximately twelve minutes. That alone prepares you, whether or not you imagine a volcanic arctic desert dotted with mountains, hot springs, and glaciers that exists in the dark for much of the year. I suspect that most of the people hearing her tone poem did just that.

In a dialogue sequence from the television series *Seinfeld* ("The Letter," 1992) Larry David wrote the following for two of his characters:

> JERRY: I have to go meet Nina. Want to come up to her loft, check out her paintings?
> GEORGE: I don't get art.
> JERRY: There's nothing to get.
> GEORGE: Well, it always has to be explained to me, and then I have to have someone explain the explanation.

In the above descriptions of Ms. Thorvaldsdottir's work, it may be helpful to pick out the word "soundscape." It indicates a kind of music that is free of melody, harmony, and rhythm and which first emerged in the 1960s. You may well ask, what's left? What's left involves masses of notes bunched up together, like the result you would get by playing the piano keyboard with a friend sitting next to you and, with your foot on the sustaining pedal, you both use your forearms (and not your fingers) to depress all eighty-eight keys simultaneously. The clusters of sounds can be achieved in different ways, but the result is the same: a rootless atmosphere of changing densities and shifting aural focal points that some people would describe as "sound design" rather than classical music. Composers like Ligeti, Penderecki, Stockhausen, and Cage brought this to the world's attention in those years, as did the 1965 world premiere of Charles Ives's Symphony no. 4 (composed between 1910 and 1924) in Carnegie Hall.

All those words in the above descriptions—"mysterious," "chaos," "enigmatic," "surreal"—appertain to works that make use of this kind of music, whether it is by John Williams for his scores to *Close Encounters of the Third Kind* and *A.I.: Artificial Intelligence,* or by Ms. Thorvaldsdottir in her *Metacosmos.* Although this style of music has been played in concerts and in film scores for over sixty years, it is still called "modern," "contemporary," or sometimes "postmodern."

And whether or not you agree with the words written by well-meaning people who want you to like this as-yet-unheard music, there is value in reading what they say to interpret the composer and her music. If it is simply confusing, always remember that you are in charge.

If you know other works by the composer of a new piece, you will, as already noted, have certain expectations, listening for the composer's brand and hearing how it has moved away from the work(s) you already know. This is a good example of something that remains the same so you can judge what is different, which is exactly the process I went through with Rachmaninoff's Symphony no. 1. There is a finite repertorial pool, of course, and only some beloved composers wrote a lot of music, as Mozart, Verdi, and Bach did. Most composers, having found their unique voice, sound like themselves, and you can judge the size and shape of their works in relation to those you know: Verdi's lesser-known *Don Carlos* against *Aïda,* Rachmaninoff's Piano Concerto no. 4 against his Piano Concerto no. 2. However, once you get to know these "firsttimers," you will tend to value these pieces for themselves and not in terms of the others.

When hearing a work for the first time, it is worth considering that composing is a little like supply-chain management. The musical elements are presented to you at a certain speed. If they come at you too fast, they fall off the conveyer belt and you will be overwhelmed with too much information. If there isn't enough information, you will become impatient and bored. Everyone is different, but the composers whose music has made it into the list of canonic works have found the sweet spot of what it is supplying and how much of it is coming at you through time. And you do not have to like it. "Bach is interesting . . . but I do not regard him as a genius," wrote Tchaikovsky in 1888.

The expression "classical music" contains within its two words an immensely varied cache of organized sound. It is rare to find a classical music lover who loves it all. Some people find early music to be the most delightful expressions of ancient times, creating in their imaginations a world of castles, minstrels, and courtly love, as well as a closeness to God in its fervent settings of religious (Christian) texts. Others cannot bear this music. "Music to commit murder by," a colleague once said. At the other end of the chronological spectrum is "modern music." This highly challenging and wildly diverse genre excites some people because of its very complex nature and the fact that it is new. Works that are not immediately comprehensible are part of what is so exciting about it. For others, it is just another block of noise.

And, amazingly enough, your judgment has nothing to do with your "training." The president of one major American orchestra did not want to program Saint-Saëns's Symphony no. 3 because he hated the piece and imposed this aversion on his audience, in spite of the fact that it is one of the most popular classical works in the repertory. The president of another major orchestra cannot wrap her brain around the standard operatic repertory. A new opera is of interest to her because of her curiosity about new works, but you won't see her at a performance of *Norma* or *Madama Butterfly*. Likewise, contemporary composers will inevitably have withering assessments of their living colleagues, as composers have frequently had in the past. The president of an important music company that publishes both old and new music recently called his latest publications "disposable music."

While that sounds shocking, because we have been taught that value is determined by a piece of music's staying power—indeed, this book is all about that—we should also be reminded once again that music before Mozart was usually a one-time affair. Its audience was site-specific, and composers never imagined it might be performed for centuries. It is possible that we may have entered another, similar era, where new classical music is just that: worthy expressions of our time that are limited to our time.

In between the two poles of early music and modern music, there are those who find Mozart boring, or Mahler to be an overblown mixture of treacle and pomposity. In their day, Rossini was embraced by many as an antidote to the rumblings and damned seriousness of Beethoven. And so, if you don't like a certain piece of classical music, you are in great company: the company of people who love classical music.

On September 7, 2018, an entire page of *The New York Times* was dedicated to eighteen artists who suggested pieces that they thought would transform you into a lover of classical music—and each within five minutes. These people wanted you to love what they love, and each of them wrote a short paragraph about why this music, above all other music, means so much to them.

What is most extraordinary is that the examples come from the entire gamut of music, starting with music by Orlando Gibbons from the early seventeenth century and ending with the contemporary music of Anna Clyne and Jessie Montgomery. In between there were works by Richard Strauss, Wagner, Beethoven, Stravinsky, Ravel, and Berlioz. The styles and contents of these works varied from stately keyboard counterpoint to complex modernism—and even included a work of total silence, John Cage's history-making *4:33*, which is in three movements, and because the performer simply sits for four minutes and thirty-three seconds, the "music" comes from the random and unpredictable sounds of the hall, its audience, and the street outside.

And there you have it: everything one might consider— with an expansive view of what constitutes classical music— covering the period from the time of Queen Elizabeth I to that of Queen Elizabeth II.

As your brain ages and your life experiences accumulate, you will hear music in an ever-evolving way. That should be neither surprising nor troubling. It is who you are. Do not be surprised if you come to Mozart when you are past fifty, or find that a new performer has given you a new experience with an old favorite. That, too, is the point. If you are concerned that the audience for classical music is aging, you should not be. Of course it is! The good news is that classical music continues to open itself to you as you age.

When my brother and I first listened to Leonard Bernstein's recording of Shostakovich's Symphony no. 5, I was fourteen years old. At that point I was already well aware of classical music but had never heard a single work by Shostakovich. Like the Russian-American Stravinsky, who was well documented in my life, the Soviet composer was alive; he had already composed eleven symphonies and would live long enough to complete fifteen before his death in 1975. He was, in other words, a contemporary composer.

The Fifth Symphony recording was released by Columbia

Records, with its logo on a gold background and the words "AN INTERNATIONAL TRIUMPH!" above the silver background with the title of the album that gave equal billing to Bernstein and the New York Philharmonic *above* the title of the work. A black-and-white photograph of the composer, the conductor, and members of the orchestra took up more than half the cover, which had the following caption, with a unique use of capitalization to express the importance of this recording: "Dimitri Shostakovitch [*sic*] and Leonard Bernstein Share an Ovation at the Historic Concert in the Bolshoi Zal of the Moscow Conservatory."

The back of the album shifted to all upper-case and red (!) in the screaming headlines of a tabloid newspaper: "AN INTERNATIONAL TRIUMPH! LEONARD BERNSTEIN NEW YORK PHLHARMONIC / SHOSTAKOVITCH SYMPHONY NO. 5." What followed was a complete list of the tour itinerary of the Philharmonic from liftoff in New York on August 3, 1959, to their return to the USA on October 13, and, as if imitating newsprint, six columns of press-release-worthy commentary and quotations about the event of an American orchestra with its American conductor having a triumph playing Soviet music in Moscow. Only at the very end, and in a small box, could I learn something about the symphony itself.

That is how I first heard this work. For a teenage boy it conveyed all the excitement and mystery of my adolescence during the Cold War. Whereas Stravinsky's new recording of his 1913 *Rite of Spring,* made the following year, in 1960, was all about pulsing and unpredictable primitive life, Shostakovich provided a journey into the gray and threatening world of contemporary Russia—even though the symphony had been composed in 1937. But this recording was clearly more than that. It was the triumph of my country over theirs. An American envelope shaped the message of a composer trapped in a totalitarian regime—and we heard it that way. The first movement's opening was like a fist raised against the oppressive policies of the government. The sunless journey of the exposition was a train to Siberia. The second movement was the fake joy engendered by vodka, and the third movement was a bleak depiction of what life must be like over there. When I first heard the thunderous stampede that was Bernstein's way with the finale, my heart raced. And I can still recall, just before the end, the slowly built cacophony, one note piling up against another, until I thought I would explode—when would this end?—just before the symphony shifts from minor mode to a major tonality of numbing and insistent triumph.

That was the winter of 1960, when I was fourteen. I first conducted the symphony in 1986 in London, and if my memory serves, it was also the first time I experienced it live. And, if that were not enough, Leonard Bernstein was in the audience.

Much had changed between being an active teenage listener of a recording and standing before the London Symphony Orchestra as a forty-year-old. For one thing, I now understood the entire arc of Shostakovich's enormous musical legacy. There would be no new works, only new interpretations and perhaps a few discoveries. My own view of the symphony had certainly broadened from a historical perspective as well as a personal one. What surprised me, as a conductor who had already worked with orchestras and opera companies throughout the world, was the toll the work took on me as a performer. The enormity of its passion is greater than anything I had predicted. A conductor, it should be said, becomes the music. Thus, for the first time, I was telling this story in a new time, before a new audience, and with a significant person within that audience who was my link to it in the first place, and who, midway between 1960 and 1986, had been my mentor—since 1971, when he had first given me advice as a twenty-five-year-old.

London orchestras frequently rehearse concerts just before their performances, with only an hour or so between the end of the final run-through and the arrival of the public. The concert, which also included works by Ives, Britten, and Bernstein, was therefore the second time the LSO and I had played the great Fifth that day. I distinctly remember that somewhere in the middle of the fourth movement of the performance, I became aware of the physical insanity of what I was doing. "I am going to die" broke through my concentration for a moment. To that, I answered, "And that's okay." Indeed, what we were doing made any sense of pain or exhaustion irrelevant. We were on a journey to life-affirming triumph, and nothing was going to stop it.

Bernstein was an immensely supportive and kind man, always sharing what he thought, and his response was both generous and sincere. I was, however, hardly done with this symphony. We conductors are perpetual students, just as those who attend concerts are always learning and adding to their knowledge. Bernstein himself changed somewhat as the years went on. Famously, the opening tempo of the last movement, which was full-on fast in 1959—much to the shock of his Soviet audience—slowed down over the decades, which allowed Bernstein to accelerate into the frenetic pulse of the movement. In my case, I have looked at the history of my century to answer some basic questions about the intent of this music.

The Fifth has been a source of much debate and discussion. The facts of its composition are generally well known. The Soviet authorities made it officially clear in 1936 that

Shostakovich's opera *Lady Macbeth of Mtsensk* (1934), with its graphic musical descriptions of whippings, strangulation, bludgeoning, and murder by rat poison, would be the end of the line for him if he continued in this vein. The composer had already completed his Symphony no. 4, and suddenly withdrew it before anyone heard it. Nineteen thirty-seven marked the height of Stalin's purges, and to this day it is unclear how many millions of people were killed during this time. Shostakovich had to make a life-and-death decision, based on the kind of music he could compose. His Symphony no. 5 is the result of that decision.

Knowing these facts is always in the back of any conductor's mind when approaching this symphony. Many people in the audience know this, too. The triumphant ending is for some a garish parody of true triumph, like an artificial Christmas tree festooned with multicolored lights. A conductor can underscore this view by drawing out the oft-repeated D-major chords and making the brass play with unpleasantly blaring sound. As to how I have evolved since I was fourteen in terms of specific interpretational approaches, what is most important when I am retelling this tale from the mid-twentieth century is how the audience understands it in the twenty-first, not how I do.

I recently heard a performance of the work with the New York Philharmonic conducted by Semyon Bychkov and was taken in by the journey, which at times was faster than my expectations. Occasionally inner voices called out from inside the work that were illuminating as well as disruptive—as they should be. The standing ovation was deserved by all. On the other hand, a colleague of mine achieved what I thought impossible with the Chicago Symphony by making the ending so unpleasant that the audience response was what I call a "leaving ovation"—people clapping as they exit.

Shostakovich knew exactly what he was doing when he hit upon a way to end his Fifth. The Soviets wanted music that was comprehensible to the public and also wanted it to end in uplift. This, in earlier times, would hardly have been an unreasonable demand from Count Esterházy, the archbishop of Salzburg—and, it should be added, from the paying public. His "correction" achieved everything he and his bosses wanted. It is no more cynical than Stravinsky's D-flat-major ending to his 1945 Symphony in Three Movements or Hindemith's E-flat-major ending to his Symphony in E-flat from 1940.

Whenever I get to a critical point in the last movement of this symphony I feel an enormous tension emanating from the music. It seems to be asking, "Where shall I go?" Up to this point, for forty minutes, the symphony has projected loneliness and despair. Its beauty is the beauty of a barren and windswept landscape, and its positive emotions rise only to the level of empathy and quiet hope that end the third movement. Those feelings are immediately erased when, after remaining silent for sixteen minutes, the brass section enters *forte* and makes a crescendo to *fortississimo*—very, very loud—while the timpani pounds out a repeated series of inflexible and barbaric eighth notes, all of which begin to accelerate, as if we were under the heels of a thousand jackboots.

A third of the way through this movement the music comes crashing to the ground and a quietly heroic theme is heard from the solo French horn. The strings sing out a song of mercy, but the answer to this prayer is elusive. For more than two minutes the symphony seems to be dissolving right before our ears. I cannot escape processing this life-and-death choice as I move through the composer's dilemma in solving the puzzle of survival and artistic truth. It is no accident that Shostakovich carried around a copy of *Hamlet* wherever he traveled and wrote no fewer than three different scores to accompany the play. "To be or not to be" was no idle quotation.

And then he hits on the idea that would save his life, the lives of his family, and ensure something he may not have imagined: he would live to compose another ten symphonies and die in his bed. It begins with the return of the snare drum in march time. I hear the composer saying, *Give them the opening notes of that military theme that started the movement, but in a different way: not as a threat but as a call of survival.* Everyone gets what he wants—including, it should be said, the public.

It is no accident that Shostakovich's Fifth is his most popular work. It is his iconic work—even if many of us are committed to everything he wrote—and one of the very last symphonies to enter the unshakable canon of masterpieces of classical music. It also created a template of success for the composer, which inevitably creates a larger aesthetic question to those of us who were brought up to hate totalitarianism and value freedom of expression. We all must confront the reality of what music from the mid-twentieth century has found its way into our concerts. Both Sergei Prokofiev's and Shostakovich's Soviet-controlled works remain vital and beloved, even as the Soviet Union has been consigned to history.

My current view of this symphony is now less attached to the Cold War and its time. Like so many great classical works, it is another hard-won progression toward resolution and fulfillment. It is a symphony of human resilience and creativity. I am not that fourteen-year-old in awe of its visceral power. It is the work's humanity that makes it timeless.

My personal journey with Shostakovich and his Fifth Symphony of course has the advantage of my being a performer, but that does not mean it is unique or any more valid than anyone else's. The audience will always get the last word when it comes to the music as well as being the ultimate interpreter of the music. New artists are continually emerging, and new ideas are constantly being proffered.

Always—*always*—give the composers and performers the benefit of the doubt. Try to understand what treasures they are presenting to you and how they do it. Each musician is different, and each is trying to solve mysteries while preserving them at the same time, as I explained above. Classical music has so much going on within it that no performance can ever present a work's totality. However, you will determine whether what we bring to each piece is sufficient to unlock enough crucial aspects of the work's greatness to justify our attempt at translating it. A subtle adjustment of internal dynamics will bring out certain musical lines within a work. A slight slowing down before a harmonic shift will cause you to take particular notice of it. There is equal justification in being fascinated by a young performer reinvigorating a beloved work as by an older master performing the same piece. You may ask of some young performer, "What does *she* know of this?" She will tell you! So much of music is about imagination and memory that a young person can conjure up age and experience, just as an older artist can re-create youth.

At age fifty-four in 2018, German violinist Anne-Sophie Mutter said: "I have a deeper understanding of music and, if you want it or not, life does leave its marks not only on your brain but in your heart and in your soul. The understanding deepens." The older musician digs inward to interpret the music with decades of experience with both the notes and life itself. The young one feels impervious and impetuously leaps outward. Both are compelling and legitimate.

When you find the music you love, you create a web of interactions with your life and with the piece of music itself.

Its connection to other pieces may surprise you. Each performance will be linked to those that came before it and will add to your knowledge and experience. And it is part of our nature to want to know more.

You may still be asking, "How do I learn?" As I said earlier, the language of Western classical music has been floating around you your entire life. People who know a lot don't always "get" it. Those who are naive to the jargon can still be enraptured by it. In Turin, a friend and I stopped in a rustic trattoria on the outskirts of town. The radio was playing Mozart and the eight-year-old son of the proprietors was sitting transfixed. His mother could not explain it. We made sure young Alessandro and his mother were admitted to rehearsals, where he heard live music for the first time. I have no idea what became of that boy, but I smile at remembering the effect music had on him.

How to improve *your* receptivity is a bit more challenging, since you cannot have a guide during a performance except when current technologies attempt to give members of the audience simultaneous program notes (on personal devices). But reading can block the ears from hearing. The brain focuses on the words and blocks the auditory centers from working at full capacity.

Sports appreciation is easier. Televised commentary makes sports a constant source of education, with experts analyzing each play in a constant stream, passing on knowledge and opinion. Slow-motion replays teach the eyes of the audience how to differentiate the moves and the strategies of athletes. It is colorful and kinetic. You probably have played at least one of those sports and understand how difficult it is to be great at it. Interviews with the athletes before and after make the experience with them personal. The athletes are turned into heroes. The evening news reports their activities as both locally and, later on, internationally important. Trophies and halls of fame are visual representations of just how much we are meant to value them and what they do. Towns, cities, and countries see their athletes as representing them on the world stage.

Music does not participate in this method of teaching and support, except by means of dedicated educational tools— something that feels like school to many and is not much fun. Thus, if you become interested in, say, a Mahler symphony, what will guide you will be information culled from reading and hearing (ideally, not at the same time). There can also be a certain unfortunate stigma that comes along for the ride. When I wrote and hosted an evening classical music program in Los Angeles, the transcripts were sent to another major classical music station to see if they wanted to broadcast the programs. The director of programming said no. Listeners wanted to hear the music and not words. "And anyway," she said, "our listeners know all that."

Classical music does not cover a vast period of time and most of it, as you know, was composed in Europe. Learn the origin stories of the music you love. If fans of the Beatles can take a tour from Liverpool to the Indra Club in Hamburg to Abbey Road Studios in London, then you can travel with your favorite classical composers in mind and partake in the environments of their music and their lives. Experience the weather in Vienna and imagine Beethoven's walks there. Visit Mendelssohn's spacious home in Leipzig, see a lock of his curly red hair in a glass case, and then drink coffee where Schumann spent time with his friends at the Arabian coffee-house, Coffe Baum, open for business since 1711. A short walk from there and you can hear music in the church where many of Bach's cantatas were first performed every Sunday morning. Hear music in Venice at the Basilica of San Marco and you will feel a direct communion with Monteverdi and Vivaldi; then stay at the palazzo that is now a hotel on the Grand Canal where Wagner died in 1883. Your imagination can and will do more than any guidebook or classroom.

Rehearsals are a great way to understand what's going on. Most symphony orchestras allow the public in, but usually that's only at a dress rehearsal when much of the work is already done. Older concert halls separate the audience from the orchestra, while newer auditoriums allow you to view the orchestra from many sides, even from behind, which allows you to view the conductor from the front.

If you know people in a chamber group, they might let you in to view the process of preparing. Most of us do not want people watching what we consider backstage preparations, as interesting as they might be for you. Unions will also see it as protection of the musicians. In years past, the outrageous and humiliating behavior of conductors encouraged the closing of these sessions to outsiders. However, the Internet is full of rehearsal videos, and this, too, can be helpful in seeing and hearing the puzzle's pieces being assembled and honed before it is all put together in performance.

The web of continuity, however, does not start at a concert or a rehearsal. The DNA of classical music is everywhere to be found: in the music that sells pharmaceuticals and life insurance on our television and video screens, in the music played by buskers in our subway and metro stations, in the music that gives life and soulfulness to computer-generated two-dimensional characters on the screen. People who love classical music will definitely want to help you love what they love. When a college student who works part-time where I get my mail was taken to the opera for the first time (*Carmen*), he said, "I was surprised that I knew all the songs." And when we get married, almost without fail, we make an adult life commitment while the music of two antagonist classical geniuses is played: Mendelssohn's wedding march from *A Midsummer Night's Dream*, and Richard Wagner's from *Lohengrin*. When Europe looked for an anthem that represented a continent, it chose Beethoven.

And when it comes to planet Earth, classical music has been celebrating it for centuries. The love of the planet represents a large portion of the repertoire, from Vivaldi to Thorvaldsdottir: the seasons, clouds, storms, stars, the sea, the dawn and the sunset, moonlight, mountains, forests, birds, deserts, oceans, a wild rose, and the craggy mountains of Iceland. Classical music will always be a great protoenvironmental art form. It and you can celebrate life and death and all the miracles in between together. We all begin our personal and collective webs without ever trying, and without ever knowing it.

Some people are troubled by a nagging question: Are you *supposed* to like it? That question has an implied shadow question. Are you supposed *not* to like it, because it's old and not cool? It is *not* cool. At some periods of time, it was "the fashion," the place to be, especially when it was commissioned by the court; but the staying power of the great works was never determined by the fashion of the times. Classical music stands as the pillar of who we are as a civilization. Chess is not cool. Neither is the Taj Mahal, the Sistine Chapel, or the Magna Carta. Classical music is not a temporary phenomenon. It is not of the moment. It is of every moment. It waits for you and welcomes you whenever you enter its domain and it enters yours.

CHAPTER 8

The Concert Experience

Norman Rockwell captured the challenge facing a young
piccolo player and his mother in this 1919 cover for *The American
Magazine*. Thousands of hours of practice and the support
of friends and family go into every musician's life.

IN THE EARLY 1950s, the American Federation of Musicians came out in a united front to "support live music." The proliferation of recorded music on vinyl long-playing records and the broadcasting of it on radio stations (the latter making high-fidelity reception, free of noise interference and with a wider bandwidth, a new and impressive option) created the fear that the public would stop hiring live musicians and would prefer instead to hear music at home, for free. By the late 1950s, FM stereo reception was approved in the United States, making the union's concern even greater. European union leaders, it should be said, did not react this way. The tradition of radio orchestras—orchestras created with the sole purpose of broadcasting—had been a normal part of state-run radio ever since the 1920s.

Technology brought sound reproduction to an unprecedented level with the development of turntables that precisely controlled the speed of the disc, lighter-than-air tone arms with diamond styluses at their tip, amplifiers and preamplifiers, and speaker systems that included tweeters, woofers, and midrange combinations that could replicate sounds that went above and below human hearing.

In many ways, there was a similar sense in the Hollywood of the 1950s when the television set became the focal point of most American living rooms, replacing the fireplace of yore, the spinet piano, and the radio console of the first half of the twentieth century. When color television emerged, it looked like the movie industry was soon to become a quaint but moribund part of cultural history.

Hollywood went on the offensive and developed wall-to-wall screens that approximated the 130-degree horizontal visual field of the human eye, making puny television screens feel more like a porthole rather than Cinerama, CinemaScope, Ultra Panavision 70, Cinemiracle, or Todd-AO, which put you on the prow of the ship. The musical scores to those films were played through multitrack stereophonic sound systems positioned behind the screen and throughout the theater. Television sets were equipped with a tiny monaural speaker that could not even compete with FM radio, forcing some television specials to have simultaneous radio broadcasts to accompany the television experience. The great symphonic scores to *Ben-Hur* (Miklós Rózsa), *The Robe* (Alfred Newman), *The Ten Commandments* (Elmer Bernstein), and *Cleopatra* (Alex North) were acoustically overwhelming, putting the audience inside the orchestra, no matter where you sat in the movie theater. I will never forget hearing, as a teenage boy, the thunderclap that accompanied Jesus's death in *The Robe* come from *behind* me with Newman's orchestra and chorus *surrounding* me.

All of this left the issue of the viability of a classical music concert an unanswered question. Facing a world in which music of every kind was accessible to anyone with a radio or a few dollars to attend a movie, organizers of the concert experience responded by keeping things exactly the same, with few exceptions. Leopold Stokowski, for instance, had experimented with colored lighting at his concerts with the Philadelphia Orchestra, but this did not inspire others to follow. Television networks occasionally put orchestra concerts and operas on the little screen, but soon found out that classical music is not particularly telegenic.

In the concert hall, the orchestra, dressed in nineteenth-century white tie and tails, still came to the stage, tuned up, stood to bow with the conductor (everyone white and male, with the possible exception of the harpists, who were nonetheless white), and then sat down to play a piece of music from that same nineteenth century. The audience sat in the dark, watching the back and the sides of the conductor, the outside stands of the violins on their left and (usually) the cellos on the right. They applauded at the end of each piece, and when it was all over, they went home.

Today, it still remains the same—though the gender and racial balance within orchestras has significantly improved. Upon further reflection, perhaps you might conclude that since orchestras and chamber music organizations are selling an invisible acoustic product, it was the only appropriate response to the technologies of the twentieth century. And you can also see why there was a sense of fear that the concert might die within a few decades, a victim of the sensorial pleasures that were everywhere to be heard and seen elsewhere.

And yet here we are, still coming together in the dark to hear acoustic music played for us by living human beings. In fact, it is the only place where you can experience acoustic music, since classical music is created and re-created by sounds coming from instruments that are made of natural elements that make the air vibrate, combining their efforts with their colleagues, and all of it creating beauty for you. Every other kind of music you hear—pop, Broadway, country, hip-hop, and your favorite recordings—is coming to you from speakers that are responding to electrical impulses that compromise, compress, add reverberation, equalize, edit, and fool the brain in one gigantic and generally acceptable simulacrum of the real thing: a person playing an instrument.

Earlier, I suggested you consider the lineage of the musical instruments that are used in classical music from the point of view of their natural components as well as the creativity, the curiosity, and the technologies in metallurgy, machinery, and engineering, that go back to prehistoric times. Now let us consider the people on the stage who are about to perform for you, and how they got there.

When children are handed a violin or an oboe, their first sounds will be something quite unexpected and not very pretty. The violinists will quickly find out, after being shown how to tighten the hair on the bow and turn the neck at an uncomfortably acute angle so that the violin can be held between the chin and the left shoulder, that drawing the bow across one of the instrument's four strings will make it bounce uncontrollably or, in the better cases, produce a sound that is something like that of the neighbor's cat.

An aspiring oboist will be instructed as to how to put the new instrument together from three pieces of shaped and hollowed blackened wood and might marvel at the complex beauty of its silver keys that flap up and down, articulated against its body. A reed is then handed to the young person. It is an odd thing, because it is actually a double reed—two blades of thinly shaped cane bound together. It is relatively short, and once it is inserted into the top part of the oboe, the child will be encouraged to place the double reed into his or her mouth, fold the lips inward, and exhale while keeping the lips sealed around the reed. With a burst of air that fights to make it through that tiny opening, there may be a sound! It will not sound like an oboe, but something like a duck that has swallowed an oboe.

And from here the journey that ends with all those musicians on the stage begins. The challenges and frustrations and uncountable hours of work—solitary and frequently thankless, but always with a goal of achieving mastery over the object in their hands and with the ultimate goal of playing *music*—may not be obvious to you. Every one of those musicians has devoted a lifetime in pursuit of harnessing a chosen instrument, wrestling with it, getting better over years of steadfast work, being mentored by teachers who scold, inspire, challenge, and enrage. Every player has an ideal sound to be striven for. Each microscopic position change, whether it is in the angle of the wrist, the position of the bow, the placement of a finger just so, will allow the young instrumentalist to get closer to the ideal that is always mysteriously just out of reach.

There is some support in this process—a community of other young musicians who play in the high-school orchestra or band, who attend recitals and concerts, competitions, summer camps, conservatories—but also an endless series of humiliating auditions until the one after which a musician is invited to be on the stage. The musicians' chosen instruments become extensions of their bodies and their souls. When the cellists walk onstage, they may not be particularly graceful, but once they sit and place their instrument between their legs, lower their shoulders, center their bodies, and draw the bow across the strings—their left cheek resting intimately against the neck of the instrument while they tune up—the instrument and the instrumentalist are transformed into a single entity of grace and balance worthy of any ballet dancer.

And none of the above mentions the learning of music itself, what it means to be faithful to its notes and their intent, and how best to get the appropriate sound to express what the musician is feeling. Whatever your aesthetic choices are regarding style and content of instrumental music, you must never forget the miracle of hard work, human achievement, aspiration, and talent that each player represents with every note he or she plays or sings.

Unless you are attending a solo recital, the final thing to consider before a note has sounded is how much must be given up and given into making music with another person. I will soon discuss various combinations of musicians you might encounter at a concert of classical music, but consider for a moment how starting from two players and progressing to numbers in the hundreds, each component player must donate into a greater good—the ensemble—through a never-ending series of compromises and telepathic communication, creating an idealized society of colleagues with the goal of giving you an invisible gift, something that will disappear within a half-second of the last note played.

The community experience of sitting together in the audience to participate in a unique ritual will never be in danger of being replaced by any technology, because it is real in every sense of the word. Here is the place where you can fully participate, where music is not background. It is a little like going to a place of worship or taking part in meditation. It can also be like attending an athletic event, because it will always be unpredictable, and even the greatest musicians are always in danger of missing a note, having a memory slip, and having a bad night. Or something transformative can happen that raises the experience and goes far beyond what Yo-Yo Ma calls "the engineering" part of making music. What they are doing is the product of truly amazing technical feats of muscle control and artfulness. Recordings, edited with ever-increasing control, have erased the dangers, the unpredictability, and are like a game in which every kick results in a goal, a highlights reel of beautiful but predictable perfection. In 1965, when Vladimir Horowitz returned to Carnegie Hall for a solo recital following twelve years of public silence, we in the audience were thrust into the electricity of a human being attempting to control his emotions and tame the eighty-eight keys of the Steinway concert grand before him.

His entrance was greeted with cheers and warm applause. Horowitz was a private man who only expressed himself through music. He barely made eye contact with us and sat down, which immediately stopped the applause. Once he had settled himself at the keyboard, he tore into Busoni's transcription of Bach's C Major Toccata—and *blam!* he hit a wrong note at the end of the first phrase. A short but ugly mess (made all the more noticeable because it is followed by silence) was a wake-up call to all of us who knew his technically perfect recordings.

In a very real way, it was the greatest thing he could have done (though I doubt he would agree). It made everything he did afterward even more remarkable and precious. And yes, there were other "mistakes," but it did not matter one bit. We were with him through it all, and his opening gaffe immediately unleashed our communal empathy. The great pianist and Ives scholar John Kirkpatrick once said, "If you can't play the notes, play the music!" And never was that more true than on that Sunday afternoon at Carnegie Hall.

When you are not Vladimir Horowitz, the challenge of wrong notes, squeaking clarinets, out-of-tune playing, a split note from the French horns, can hit a tipping point. Music can be a stern taskmaster.

When you attend amateur concerts there will always be the challenge of hearing the music in spite of technical errors. A high-school orchestra's performance can be challenging. The problem is that when something is out of tune, there is an immediate and involuntary visceral response to the sound of it. Sometimes, as was the case with the delusional American socialite Florence Foster Jenkins (memorably portrayed onscreen in 2016 by Meryl Streep), the Australian comedienne Anna Russell, or the Portsmouth Sinfonia (a student group that reputedly enlisted players with little or no ability), incompetent attempts at singing or playing great classical music can be the source of laughter.

And there is also the matter of just how much slack you the listener want to grant a performer. Birgit Nilsson was the greatest Wagnerian soprano of the second half of the twentieth century, and yet some people could not listen to her because she frequently sang sharp—i.e., a little higher than the intended note. Leonard Bernstein, on a particularly grumpy day in 1977, attended a performance of students from the University of Indiana in which the comely clarinetist let out a dreadful squeak during a performance of Schubert's "The Shepherd on the Rock," for soprano, clarinet, and piano. To the surprise of everyone within earshot, Bernstein said, "It could happen to anybody."

Many of the greatest musical experiences I have had have been with university orchestras. The sense of commitment and discovery is palpable. These young musicians are learning about team building, interdependency, and intentionality. There is never a bored or boring moment when an entire orchestra is playing a Brahms symphony for the first time. Most of these young people will not become professional musicians, but their time in an orchestra will have trained them for many of the challenges in the lives ahead of them.

During a performance of Danny Elfman's Violin Concerto with the Stanford University Symphony Orchestra, something went seriously wrong in the middle of the very complex second movement. The music was unraveling and required a quick decision. Without saying a word, I stopped conducting and let the players continue playing until I lifted my hands to the next structural place in the score. Without my saying a word, and with a telling look, everyone jumped to that place and all was righted.

Two things came of that moment. First of all, the players probably had never experienced that kind of group think. "Why did we know to do that?" one astonished student said later on. The other was a certain fearlessness that followed. They knew that the worst thing had almost just happened. We did not stop. For the next half hour they played quieter, louder, more rhythmically and insightfully, impervious to any danger anyone thought possible. Theirs was a truly great performance and a powerful lesson for all of us. The audience, which was hearing the work for the first time and had no point of comparison, nonetheless knew something extraordinary was happening, and the level of rapt attention only increased the sense of occasion, culminating in a standing ovation.

No matter what kind of concert you attend, it is important to remember that the total experience is made up of a composite of smaller elements. Song recitals can contain upwards of two dozen art songs, all put together in groups and proceeding toward the end—with pleasurable encores at the ready. Orchestra concerts are frequently built around a soloist who will play a "standard" concerto, to which is added a modern work that might be receiving a local or world premiere.

Metacosmos opened the April 4, 2018, New York Philharmonic concert and was followed by Beethoven's Piano Concerto no. 3, composed in 1800, with soloist Benjamin Grosvenor. After intermission, the Philharmonic and Esa-Pekka Salonen performed Beethoven's Symphony no. 3, the *Eroica*, completed in 1804. This, emphasizing what I said previously, I believe, makes hearing—actually hearing—the contemporary music especially difficult. If you were curating an art museum, it is unlikely you would hang a small contemporary painting next to two large works that came from the era of Napoleon and expect more than the most peripheral assessment of the brand-new work. More than likely, it would be considered a random choice.

When the art historian Everett Fahy reorganized New York's Metropolitan Museum of Art's collection and also repainted the walls in various dark colors in 1971, he was interviewed by *The New Yorker*. "The most common reaction, even from people who have been here thirty years, is that we've cleaned the pictures," he said. "But it's the dark backgrounds—they've removed the old masters' dinginess and given the paintings a kind of rich glow." He added, "Our Impressionist paintings now look the way people thought they did in the nineteenth century." He was also praised for organizing the collections so as to project historical continuity. Art exhibitions are like real estate, where the rule of thumb is simple: location, location, location. That is also true in how you hear a piece of music within a concert program.

Symphonic concerts are usually built from three different pieces of music, and how they relate—indeed, the order of the same pieces—will affect how you perceive them. If you start a concert with, say, Beethoven's Fifth it will feel completely different from ending part one with it or indeed building the concert so that it is the grand conclusion of the evening. Beethoven himself organized the Fifth Symphony's world premiere to be the last work on the concert, one that began with the world premiere of his Symphony no. 6. In other words, a concert is a new piece of music built from a series of pieces; at least that is how you will experience it.

Many things go into the construction of a concert, involving a soloist (and what the soloist is offering that season), popular works that have not been performed for a number of seasons, rehearsal time (challenging new works take up time and standard works can usually be brought back with a minimum of rehearsal), the desires and the reputation of the conductor, and the demands of the marketing department.

In the late 1960s and early 1970s, I experimented with concert construction based on studies in brain function, language theory, and an especially fascinating field called psychoacoustics. All of these studies concern what you, the audience, are hearing and perceiving, not what we composers and performers are doing, or think we are doing. At that time, I was the sole artistic director of a great student volunteer orchestra, the Yale Symphony. I suppose no one ever had more freedom than we had then, even though the checks and balances would be obvious from one rehearsal to the next. If a clarinetist hated the music, or didn't buy into the programmatic idea, he/she could just hand in a resignation. If we did not persuade the public (mostly busy undergraduates) to trust us, they simply did not show up.

Of course, we made some mistakes, like preceding Schoenberg's epic cantata *Gurrelieder* with the American premiere of Debussy's Music for *King Lear*. I thought having a curtain raiser was important (wrong!) and that performing two works that were composed at the same time, but with different aesthetics, would be both successful and interesting (wrong and maybe). The Debussy was the musical equivalent of a flea on an elephant, and completely forgotten about five minutes into the Schoenberg.

On the other hand, when we performed Bruckner's final symphony, the incomplete Ninth, we preceded it with Wagner's Prelude to *Tristan und Isolde,* with its concert ending. The concert had no intermission. The Wagner set a speed of information and a density of harmonies that prepared the audience for Bruckner's stately musical language. Since Wagner's concert ending is almost never played (you are likely to hear the prelude linked to the so-called *Liebestod*), it made for a pseudo first movement of a new composite work: one movement by Wagner followed by three by Bruckner—who worshiped Wagner. The last completed movement begins with a melody that sounds very much like a variation on the opening melody of *Tristan*, which therefore acted as a frame for the entire concert.

Some of my young colleagues thought this was a terrible idea. "It's like serving boiled potatoes with mashed potatoes," one said. Perhaps you think that, too, subscribing to the idea that concerts should be more of a variety pack. Exploring the tastes and textures of the potato, however, might have a place in the concert hall.

That same season we performed a concert called "The Three Faces of Stravinsky." Stravinsky, it should be pointed out, was very much alive at the time. The idea was to take his first and last ballets and play them with one of the middle-period ballets, and in chronological order. Stravinsky, as I said, changed his style—his brand, as it were—more than any other composer we hold within the pantheon of greats. The program consisted of his most popular work, a suite from his 1910 score to *The Firebird*, followed by the 1937 *Jeu de cartes* (Card Game), amusingly called "a ballet in three deals," and ending with his foray into twelve-tone composition, *Agon*, from 1957. Once again, one of my young colleagues said, "You are, of course, going to end with *Firebird*." I thought not. I liked the experiment of taking all of us (me included) in a compressed time frame: forty-seven years in a composer's life in a little over an hour.

The opening work was known to just about everyone. The second work had a tartness, like a musical game of funhouse mirrors with parodistic quotations from the standard repertory of the past. The advantage of playing this score in concert is that each of the "three deals" begins with the same music, so a first-time listener knows how to navigate the journey. *Agon* was the most challenging, because Stravinsky had abandoned his Rimsky-Korsakov beginnings and his piquant neoclassical period by the 1950s. Most important, *Agon* was almost brand new. It was the Stravinsky of our day, the Stravinsky who had recently moved to New York City. *Agon* is made up of a series of short dances, with an opening fanfare that is repeated at the end, giving it a frame—helping a first-time listener—and it is about the same durational time as the other two works.

Did it work? I hope so. As an encore (whether demanded or not) we affixed the composer's ballet "for a young elephant," the *Circus Polka* from 1942. In other words, another ballet score (a very short one) from the middle period, where we left the audience smiling.

Esa-Pekka Salonen had a very different approach in presenting an all-Stravinsky concert a few years ago. The first half contained Stravinsky's works for solo piano and orchestra, and the second half was a complete performance of *The Firebird*, as opposed to the suite. This concert was sold out at the performance I attended at Lincoln Center. About five minutes into the program, I was aware of a curious whooshing sound all around me. The audience, having realized that they were dropped into very difficult musical waters, had simultaneously opened their programs (the whoosh I was hearing) and were dutifully reading as the music continued. After intermission, a colorful and dramatic performance of *The Firebird* repaid their patience, and they responded with a standing ovation.

Michael Tilson Thomas once said he dreamed of playing Sibelius's Symphony no. 4 followed immediately with his Symphony no. 5. Again, this would be a fantastic journey for all concerned: going from the Fourth's dark dystopian view and into the sunlight of the Fifth. Sibelius wrote to a friend while composing its finale that "God is opening his doors for a moment, and his orchestra is playing the Fifth Symphony." Would anyone dare let us do an all-Sibelius concert with two short intermissions, starting with the naive and merry Symphony no. 3, and continuing with 4 and 5? What a privilege it would be to give or attend that concert of three twentieth-century symphonies by one composer in one evening!

All of the above gives you a window into some of the variables that go into creating concerts and concert programming, even though many of the choices are out of the hands of the performers. Ultimately, you will determine what you like and what you do not. Putting three very different works on the same program is the current go-to idea, hoping that there is at least one work that will attract you to buy a ticket. The biggest draw to the largest number of people is a famous soloist playing a work from the classical music canon. Among other things, most of this music is in the public domain: orchestras and instrumental groups can perform it without incurring performance fees from publishers and rights holders.

Since you are not the constructor of the concerts you attend, it is worth taking a moment to prepare yourself for the different kinds of music you will be hearing. As I said earlier, you are allowed not to like everything you hear. Occasionally, you will read a review of the concert you experienced that supports your impressions or makes you feel as if you and the writer were at two different concerts—and that is true. The music being played was being interpreted by two different brains that came to two different conclusions. That is the point. A great performance, mind you, occurs when everyone in the audience gives in to the experience and actually joins in the performance, much the way fans at a tennis match can energize a player. Those are rare and glorious moments.

A final word about attending a concert and not liking a piece of music: Whenever I have been asked to conduct music I have disdained, I start by asking myself, Why does this piece of music exist? The answer is not always easily available to me, but because it is my job, I must find out. This was as true with Gounod's *Faust* as it was with John Cage's *Atlas Eclipticalis*—the former feeling superficial and the latter merely interesting or, much worse, like chicanery.

Once I entered Gounod's opera from the vantage point of a Catholic homily on prurience, purity, and redemption—which was never intended to encompass the complete epic poem of Goethe—and the latter as a primary example of alternative ways to compose, cocreate, and find inspiration from the patterns of stars as seen from earth and translating them into sound, I became a convert and an enthusiastic salesman. You may not wish to devote the time to pursue understanding what you do not immediately like. However, certain works will make you curious, falling somewhere between attraction and rejection. Here is a doorway that is not locked, and pursuing this music might become a most rewarding journey.

Finally, there is the question of how you process music you have heard many times. You may need a break from another *Symphonie fantastique*, but a new conductor or a visiting orchestra can change *Fantastique* fatigue into astonishment. No one ever knows enough in classical music and, oxymoronically, everyone always knows enough. Every time a musician, whether a solo recitalist or a conductor standing before the immense forces of Mahler's Symphony no. 8, makes a tempo choice at the very top of a work, that tempo has eliminated a vast number of choices and therefore thousands of details that will not be acoustically available. At the same time, it will illuminate surface, middle, and background elements in unique ways.

Western music's temporal world is a little like the way a strobe light works on a record turntable. If you speed classical music up, the fast notes might disappear or be smudged and you will find yourself hearing the middle voices and the bass notes that ground the harmonic motion of everything above it. In this curious way, faster performances can feel slower, since both the middle and lower elements generally move at a slower pace than the top. Conversely, slowing down will bring the faster notes to the front of your perception, making slower seem faster. A good example of this is the andante of Beethoven's Ninth Symphony. The standard tempos taken by conductors will focus on the top line of music. If a conductor chooses to follow Beethoven's metronome markings, which ask for a significantly faster tempo, the focus shifts and transforms what is usually heard as the melody into a filigree that acts as an ornament to the slower melody just beneath the surface.

In addition, the acoustics of the hall will make tempo adjustments of the performers essential to hearing each other and communicating the music to you. Many people noted that Toscanini's broadcasts and recordings with the NBC Symphony that took place in the custom-built Studio 8H—now a television studio—were fast and brittle, whereas his performances with the Philadelphia Orchestra from the same period were more expansive and supple. This primarily had to do with acoustics. All music is a dialogue with the hall, and many of us look at the hall as the ultimate instrument we must play in order to get the music to you in the audience as we wish it to sound. My recordings of *Candide* with the New York City Opera and *Street Scene* with the Scottish Opera are both a good deal slower than my performances in the theater because of the reverberant acoustics of the Manhattan Center and Govan Town Hall, where they were recorded. In order to hear the words from the singers and allow the orchestra to hear each other in fast passages, tempos had to be moderated. (Listeners think that recordings are made in theaters and concert halls linked to the name of the orchestra or the opera company. This is generally not the case except for live-performance recordings.)

A symphony played in a cathedral is quite different acoustically and visually from that same symphony played in a concert hall. Concert halls vary from the old shoebox shape, the even older half-circled balconies with a raised stage seen from below by those in the orchestra stalls, and the more recent wraparound style that started in 1963 with Berlin's Philharmonie. The color of the interior will affect the way you concentrate and therefore how you hear. When Philharmonic Hall opened Lincoln Center in 1962, its walls were a deep midnight blue. The seats, the balcony surfaces, and the acoustical "clouds" above our heads were in various shades of gold. Erasing any sense of the city outside, that extraordinary room remains one of the most beautiful interiors—long gone—I have ever experienced. Even the lighting will change not only how you hear and your attention to the performance (reading program notes will assign part of your body budget away from listening) but also the ritual of coming together and sitting in the dark for a common sensory experience.

Classical music is not elitist, but it can make you feel grand because of where you experience it and what you are hearing, inhabiting some sumptuously appointed spaces of a bygone era. The music itself might take us deep into the environs of dreams. We are there to pay a small percentage of the costs of having such a privilege in which the greatest musicians in the world perform just for us at that moment and in that hall.

We enter an agreement of imaginary privilege and grandeur otherwise impossible to sustain beyond a few hours. As I wrote at the very beginning of this book, we exit having shared in the pretending and then we get into public transportation or our cars and return to wherever we live, having broken through class, race, and economic barriers to voluntarily join with strangers in the hopes of becoming one with them through music.

The old Metropolitan Opera House had a separate side-door entrance for people in the least expensive seats: the euphemistically called Family Circle. The "poor people" got in an elevator that made only one stop, the top balcony, which had no access to those in the rest of the hall. Even under such impossibly exclusionary conditions, those of us who sat there experienced something magnificent, and knew we also had the best acoustical position in the red-and-gold palace.

With all those variables in mind, it is important to know that classical music concerts range in size and shape, length and width, complexity, darkness and light. You therefore have many options to enter and explore the canon as you please. Some may feel unwelcome at a symphony concert or feel there is a requirement to dress up out of a sense of respect and formality for classical music. On the other hand, some people prefer to dress up for a special occasion and are more comfortable not wearing blue jeans. All of this is understandable and a personal choice.

No matter how you dress—and sometimes the venue encourages the level of formality or informality—you might want to experience the many kinds of live concerts that classical music offers. What follows here is a brief overview and a guide.

The Solo Recital

A solitary human stands alone before you with an instrument in hand or a grand piano awaiting. The piano recital, for example, allows you to directly feel the power and the genius of one person at the great keyboard instrument of our time. Composers from the entire classical music period have composed for the keyboard. Some of the music is for children; some was intended for amateur playing in one's home; some was composed for the magicians of the instrument, who could make you forget that every sound was coming from two hands, ten fingers, and two feet.

The piano recital is an opportunity to experience a direct link with the hands of the master composers, who, almost without exception, composed at the keyboard. Those were Beethoven's hands, Debussy's hands, Rachmaninoff's hands. The piano was a playground for experimentation in expression and private exploration. The living musician's hands can also be seen as an instrument, molded and trained through thousands of hours of private practice. And since so many people have an early experience playing the piano, you will directly understand the extraordinary facility, technical mastery, and raw talent that pianists offer to us.

One of the astounding discoveries will be the different qualities of sound that pianists can draw from what is essentially an enormously complex, hand-operated machine. The touch on the keys, the use of the pedals (there are three), and the weight of the arms will all affect the sounds you will hear. In a way, it is very much like the many ways a tennis player or a golfer addresses the ball, only in this case there are eighty-eight keys and those keys are attached to hammers that strike multiple strings for each note.

The other aspect of a piano is that we can classify it as a percussion instrument. Any note you play can only do one thing once it is struck: decay. Unlike notes played on a violin or a trumpet, notes on a piano simply die away, and the effect of great crescendos or smooth legato has everything to do with the artistry of the pianist, how they link each note to the preceding ones and how making use of the sustaining pedal allows the strings to vibrate longer while also causing other strings to vibrate sympathetically with the note that has been struck.

Beethoven composed thirty-two sonatas, and spending your life with these masterpieces alone would be a sufficient partner in anyone's lifetime. They seem to encompass a universe of expression and experience, and every pianist who attempts them will illuminate something new and familiar at the same time. Beethoven used his sonatas to grab your attention with their dramaturgy and surprises. Hearing them in a small auditorium, or in someone's home, can be a life-enriching experience.

On the other hand, Mozart's piano sonatas will delight you, and Debussy's solo piano works will lead you into wafting aromas from non-European shores. As pianist Stephen Hough so perceptively wrote in *The New York Times*, Debussy's absorption with exoticism "[went] to the marrow. It [was] a transfusion of blood, flowing in the very fingers which conjure up these new sounds at this old instrument . . . [His] discovery of new sounds at the piano is directly related to the physiology of hands on keyboard. It is impossible to conceive of most of Debussy's piano music being written at a desk, or outdoors, despite his frequent use of 'en plein air' titles."

All this awaits you at a piano recital. This is also true of a solo organ recital, though the connection with the player is much harder to achieve, since the keyboard might be hidden from view in a church or the console might require the artist to sit with his/her back to you.

When an instrumentalist or a singer is joined by a piano and there are two people before you, the solo recital becomes something else, because you experience the art of accompaniment— the give-and-take of who is leading and who is supporting the other. This is the essence of the art of interdependence commingled with the bravery of a person to stand before you and fearlessly tell you what she thinks. Because of its simplicity, and intimacy, the solo recital is about as personal and intense a musical experience as you can get.

The Chamber Music Concert

The word "chamber" is easily misunderstood, since it is not used much in contemporary English. Once you think about its meaning—"room," as in living room—your comfort level changes. This is music for a small group of instrumentalists playing for each other in someone's living room or parlor or, as has become customary, in a small auditorium. The pity is that so much of it was written for you to *play* as you listened. Whatever part you took was an element in a magnificent and enjoyable puzzle. Without you, the work did not exist. You were in a constant process of discovery and delight, sharing a composite sound with a few friends. You did not have their parts, only your own. As you progressed through each movement you suddenly found that you had a big solo, and that it echoed a phrase someone else had just played. Then you were in a position to accompany another colleague whose part went off in another direction. How would you all return to a sense of cohesion when you arrived at the last bar? And you had the answer to that question as you turned to the last page of your part, reading the notes just before you played them, moving inexorably toward the end and knowing before it sounded in the air, the end of your journey together with your fellow musicians.

Today, we are most likely to experience chamber music in the concert hall, perhaps with a world-famous string quartet performing brilliantly *for* us. This inevitably will be a note-perfect and highly worked-out performance of something they have played and prepared for hundreds of hours. Their united perception of the work will be a convincing representation of the composer's intent translated by a collective compromise.

"Compromise" has become something of a negative word in political, religious, and philosophical thought. Music, though, cannot exist without it, and chamber music is ground zero for how it works. Once music expands to orchestral music, led by a conductor, how that compromise is achieved changes. As one player described it, the difference between playing chamber music and orchestral music is the difference between being a landowner and being a serf.

Recently, pianist Emanuel Ax discussed rehearsing the Brahms Piano Trio no. 3 in C Minor with cellist Yo-Yo Ma and violinist Leonidas Kavakos. He said, "When we work on a piece, Yo-Yo will start out and say, 'This should be like the sunrise, and that should be like the sunset.' And I start out by asking, 'How come on the fourth beat there's a dot, and there's no dot on the third beat?' Eventually we come together, and I begin to see the sunrise, and I get him to check the dot."

If there is a composer whose music you love, there is no better way of getting up close than through chamber music, and if you are fortunate enough to hear it in a small room where you can see the players, you will instantly be pulled into it as a coperformer. You will feel the effort and see the players pass the musical elements from one to another. You will watch them making eye contact and communicating through breaths, body language, and telepathy.

Although I have enjoyed many performances of the music of John Adams, and experienced the personal challenge of conducting it, nothing prepared me for hearing his 1995 *Road Movies* at New York's chamber-music venue Le Poisson Rouge in 2015. The room holds fewer than 700 attendees, with a maximum of 250 seated, and being close to violinist Robert McDuffie and pianist Elizabeth Pridgen created the perfect environment for experiencing this breathtaking music. The audience was held emotionally hostage to these two consummate artists as they navigated Adams's rhythmic and harmonic voyages that describe how it feels to be riding in a car. The volatile combination of the music, the two performers, and the audience was something that could never have been experienced in a large concert hall or on a recording.

If you live near a music school, experiencing chamber music played by students means you are part of their discovery, too. They are polyamorous, assigned various partners by their professors, and express the deepest sense of the original purpose of chamber music—a few people sharing in process and discovery. We will always treasure the professional trios and quartet ensembles—the adults who tour and take up residencies. They get to know their partners and what their choices are probably going to be. They can prepare and adjust to the smallest nuance of their colleagues. The students, by contrast, are still learning how to play well with others.

The Choral Concert

The first instrument is the human body: its voice. Collecting groups of humans to sing together brings us to the very beginning of the human desire to expand our single voice into an idealized society of expression making use of nothing more than ourselves, giving in to a collective society that breathes, thinks, and communicates together. This can be a quartet of voices or a chorus of hundreds. Here, too, is an opportunity for many who do not play an instrument to experience the society of putting breath into the dormant outlines of notes, rhythms, and words in which everyone breathes and enunciates precisely together, becoming a single, superhuman entity.

A subset of the choral concert is the children's chorus concert, which takes the above vision of a society committed to nothing more than making beauty together to another level of emotion. The "commitment of the innocents" arouses a profound emotion of nostalgia and hope. Their idealized and pure voices remind us of halcyon days, mostly out of reach for adults, except when we hear children sing.

The Symphonic Experience

The Western orchestra is perhaps the greatest instrument ever created. It has developed from many sources, adding instruments, adapting older instruments, accepting new instruments from non-European cultures, and achieving a complex mechanism of expression that is acoustic and infinitely adaptable: loud, soft, fast, slow, high and low. The symphony orchestra for classical music requires the greatest combinations of different instruments and brilliantly skilled musicians to play them.

You may not have thought about this, but the modern symphony orchestra kept developing until the early twentieth century. By that time, the various component parts had not only been added and balanced, the development of the instruments themselves had achieved a level of perfection that needed very little adjustment, and those adjustments came mainly from certain players and conductors who created the sound we have come to expect. It wasn't until Mozart visited Mannheim, Germany, in 1777 that he encountered something he had never thought of before: using clarinets in his orchestra. It was in Mannheim that the foundational sections of the modern orchestra were created, with strings, brass, woodwinds, and timpani. The young composer wrote to his father, "Ah, if only we had clarinets too in Salzburg! You cannot imagine the glorious effect of a symphony with flutes, oboes and clarinets."

In the mid-nineteenth century, Wagner was tinkering with expanding the brass section for his *Ring* operas by adding a bass trumpet and *Tuben,* known today as Wagner tubas, though these unusual instruments, along with the bass oboe and the contrabass clarinet, never made it past a few orchestrations. With the compositions of Mahler, Strauss, and Puccini, the orchestra became a sufficient vehicle for the fantasies of most composers. Only the kinds of percussion instruments continued to grow during and after the nineteenth century, which, along with the harp, added new color combinations. The total number of players in a symphony orchestra could be expanded to reach 150 players, as for Schoenberg's *Gur-relieder,* but the component parts are the same as a symphony by Brahms or Beethoven.

Experimentation with direct imitation of sounds was an occasional element in operas and subsequently in descriptive tone poems. Thus, in Donizetti's 1835 *Lucia di Lammermoor,* some scenes require extramusical sounds—a church bell, a thunder sheet, and Benjamin Franklin's invention, the treadle-operated series of wineglasses of various sizes that emitted an unearthly sound and was known as the glass armonica—but the score is still built on woodwinds, brass, a harp, percussion, and strings.

Then there is the concerto experience. The concerto is usu-ally the "star" feature of most classical concerts, and it is a combination of the solo recital and a symphonic work. The difference (besides the obvious one of size) has to do with the relationship of the conductor with the soloist. Few people realize that no matter how a concerto sounds, the difficulty of accompanying a soloist can vary wildly. Leonard Bernstein once said of Tchaikovsky's Violin Concerto as opposed to his Piano Concerto no. 1, "One is easy. The other is hard." You probably would not have any idea of that, but every con-ductor knows how fiendishly difficult it is to accompany the piano concerto. This has to do with the way it is notated on the page and the many ways a pianist deals with its technical challenges. The violin concerto, on the other hand, is far more straightforward.

When a pianist is accompanying a violin soloist, the two musicians have spent many hours discussing every twist and turn of the music and its interpretation. That same soloist for a concerto might meet the conductor for the first time at the dress rehearsal. Not only must the conductor be prepared for as many interpretive possibilities as one could imagine, the orchestra must also be following along. Consider, for a moment, how little of a piano's sound can be heard by the trombones who are inevitably sitting in the back of the stage and facing the fully raised piano lid, which projects the soloist's sound away from them.

The battle of sounds and the balancing of them between the solo performer and a full symphony orchestra is another task that is never felt in a recital. Some composers were particularly good at considering how loud a solo cello is (not very) and others simply wrote an idealized concerto, leaving the mechanics of balancing it to the conductor. Anyone who has had to manage Dvořák's beloved Cello Concerto knows precisely what I mean. That said, when it all works, it can be the most exciting David-and-Goliath experience imaginable, and in the best-case scenario, both come out as winners.

Ballet

The two remaining classical music genres involve equal parts of seeing and hearing. Dance is the silent art based on the human form that attempts to defy the physical laws of gravity while insisting on the human form's grace and balance. You will not be the first to focus on the artists onstage and not have enough sensory bandwidth to pay attention to the music emanating from the orchestra pit or, more frequently, from speakers playing a recording of an orchestra.

That said, the greatest ballets are founded on great music, whether that is *Swan Lake* or *Agon*. When a choreographer understands the ebb and flow of the music, its harmonic and rhythmic motion, something remarkable is achieved, whether or not the dance is overtly telling a story. Unfortunately, in America many ballet companies cannot afford to put musicians in a pit, creating a straitjacket for the dancers, who must dance to a recording.

Great ballet scores are frequently played in symphonic concerts, leaving the narrative and/or the synchronized onstage movements to the audience's imagination. Story ballets remain the scores in the classical canon, and like incidental music to plays, such as Mendelssohn's *A Midsummer Night's Dream*, these are more likely to appeal to the greatest number of people. Prokofiev's music to *Romeo and Juliet* from 1938 is one of the last works of the genre to secure a place in the core classical music repertory.

Opera

Opera is the messy, complex, and ultimate expression of Western art. It was invented around 1600 to include all the arts, and its key ingredient is music, which holds it all together. There is no opera in the canon that is there for any other reason than its musical score. Leoncavallo composed a *Bohème* and Paisiello wrote a *Barber of Seville*, but it is the music of Puccini and Rossini that remain on our operatic stages.

If a composer chose to write in multiple genres—unlike Wagner and Puccini, who essentially only composed for the stage—opera is a key to understanding a composer's intent in his other works, like his symphonies, sonatas, and concertos. Beethoven's music for *Fidelio*—and how he musicalizes courage, hope and fear, light and dark—helps us understand what his *Eroica* and his Piano Sonata no. 23 (*Appassionata*) are all about. The way Beethoven describes the cold underground prison at the start of act 2, the music he uses to express hope—specifically under the words "Komm, Hoffnung" (Come, hope)—and unspeakable joy ("O namenlose Freude"), are keys to the lexicon of his instrumental music. Opera can therefore act as the Rosetta Stone of meaning for classical music.

While the vast majority of works you will hear in classical music concerts end in joy, as I have already pointed out, the canonic operatic works contain many tragic tales—especially in nineteenth century and early twentieth century Italian operas. Whereas Mozart composed an uplifting moral epilogue to his *Don Giovanni,* there is no uplift at the end of Verdi's three middle-period masterpieces *Rigoletto, Il trovatore,* and *La traviata,* which end in a murder, an execution, and the death of a reformed prostitute from tuberculosis. The canvas on which opera is painted led the way for even more unpleasantness in the twentieth century. When Beethoven set the story of a husband and wife under political strife engineered by a heartless political rival, his *Fidelio* ended with the hero's rescue by his wife and a chorus of rejoicing. When Puccini set a similar story in 1900, his *Tosca* ends with all three principals dead.

It is true that Greek tragedy—the inspiration for the invention of opera, after all—ends with murder and suicide, those works evoked a curious purging of the public through what Aristotle called catharsis. German operas in the nineteenth century, specifically those of Wagner, achieve catharsis, rather than the horror of a father discovering that the sack he is carrying around contains his daughter whom he inadvertently has had murdered, as *Rigoletto* does. However, the nineteenth-century operas that set tragic texts, like Donizetti's *Lucia di Lammermoor* and just about everything Verdi chose, dealt with moral issues and were not simply there to shock the public.

Opera is where words attached to classical music transform implication into specification. These masterpieces deal with racism, political corruption, imperialism, sexual hypocrisy, and freedom. In many cases Verdi was a political activist, and often his plots made it past the Italian censors only by being transposed to countries far from Italy, though no one needed a map to understand what his operas were saying.

Opera is very much like a high religious ritual without its taking place in a church, mosque, or temple. Operas can be tragic, comic, melodramatic, epic, stately, or fleet. However, they are always *about* something bigger than the story. Unlike other classical music, which exists in two time periods, operas take place in *three:* the time and place of the dramatic action, the time and place of its composition, and today. When you attend a performance of Richard Strauss's *Elektra,* you are experiencing a Greek play by Sophocles from around 400 BC, adapted by the Austrian Hugo von Hoffmansthal in 1903, that was again adapted by him and Strauss in 1909 that is being interpreted (staging, lighting, singing, conducting) for you by a group of people who are committed to respecting the past and simultaneously translating it for you today. This multi-century dialogue is part of opera's power.

The important thing to remember—and this is obvious to opera lovers—is that not all operas are the same. The variables within the genre are vast, whether that has to do with length, form, relationship between the orchestra's function with the voices, and the level of action required. Opera is not realistic, but rather goes beyond that into profound realms of storytelling.

However, we should not expect our operatic heroines and heroes to look like idealized physical representations of our imagination. Madame Butterfly says she is fifteen years old.

No Japanese teenager could or should ever sing the role, because of its huge physical demands. Puccini uses a large orchestra and expects his title character to be heard without amplification. In other words, two small muscles in the throat of the singer are vibrating and resonating in her sinus cavities so that she can be heard by thousands of people while acting in a costume and commanding your attention. There was no more impressive Butterfly than, in the 1960s, Leontyne Price, a great African-American soprano who was well into her thirties at the time.

People sometimes make fun of big-bodied opera singers, as if the *real* Tristan and Isolde of history were built like the superheroes of comic books or the movies. Who has the temerity to say that big people cannot fall hopelessly in love and that we in the audience can't accept that? And here, ultimately, is the point. It is the voice that represents the heart and soul of any character in an opera. Of course, we dress them up and put them in a set that gives them an environment of some kind that speaks to the time and place or the intent of the director, who may want to reinterpret the profound nature of the tale to make a specific point. The story itself usually remains, and the reason for telling it with music will usually pass through the interpretive licenses taken.

The fact that extraordinary humans are projecting all the emotions of the human experience through their voices, without amplification, should be reason enough for anyone to go to the opera. In addition, operas embody a total vision of our humanity, even when they tell stories of gods and goddesses. Because of the curious effect that adding music to a story brings to the theatrical experience, you will find yourself subconsciously empathizing with everyone onstage and interpreting them as aspects of yourself. All of the characters in

Mozart's *Don Giovanni* are roles we have played or imagined playing: the seducer, the lover, the victim, the protective parent, the underpaid and unappreciated assistant, the avenger, the unapologetic perpetrator, the moral teacher. The same is true of the characters in *Butterfly* and *Tristan*. The closer opera gets to the primal human stories, the closer we come to recognizing ourselves in everyone within it.

You should not trouble yourself, therefore, with questions of foolish reality. The entire edifice is gloriously fake and yet tells a truth that goes beyond the spoken dramas you will see onstage, on television, and in the movies.

Unlike a ballet, an opera will not be performed with a recorded orchestra. In some cases, small touring companies and schools might perform one with a piano accompaniment, which will allow young singers to attempt roles in small venues without hurting themselves by singing over a full orchestra. This, too, is important, because the human voice is a fragile thing, and misusing it, like misusing any part of the human body, can cause irreparable damage.

The window of time in which a singer can successfully perform a role is shockingly small, and opera fans will see the debuts and farewells of many great artists within their own lifetimes. As the great American opera singer and teacher Phyllis Curtin said, "Every opera singer dies twice." We who love this art form know never to put off seeing a great opera singer. Within the family of classical musicians, opera singers are our most precious, heroic, and vulnerable, and experiencing them live is a privilege.

CHAPTER 9

Your Playlist, Your Life

Partnership is a fundamental part of most musicians' lives.
This 1850 daguerreotype is of Robert Schumann and his wife,
Clara—who was the greater pianist, a composer,
and a devoted supporter of her husband.

CENTENARIES PROVIDE an excellent opportunity to judge and reconsider the impact certain people have had on society. In the case of conductors and other musical performers, their legacy necessarily fades because we are merely translators. Who remembers Hans von Bülow or Mary Garden, two of the most important performers of their time, musicians who gave world premieres of works we have come to love and, perhaps more important, whose art inspired composers like Tchaikovsky and Debussy to entrust them with bringing their latest works to the public? Recordings can extend the life of performers but ultimately translations become less relevant as time goes by, because we need living embodiments of music, as much as we might respect our ancestors.

Composers' centenaries are another issue. It is their music that either matters or has been judged unworthy of current reconsideration. You cannot simply create an exhibition to re-evaluate a lifetime of composing music, as you can with visual art. You cannot hang a symphony on a wall. Thus, it is a matter for classical institutions to decide if they are willing to spend time and money for such celebrations. Birthdays of some composers (Beethoven, Mozart, Schubert) are celebrated or at least marked by the media every year, whether or not the birthday is divisible by ten. Some important composers, such as Bernard Herrmann and Erich Wolfgang Korngold, had their centenaries overlooked in the United States; and Korngold's, in 1997, was marked in Vienna, his former home, by a single commemorative concert. A centenary is a good measure of just what "we" think of a composer's music, because although the composer is no longer living, many people who knew him or her and championed the works are still alive. Younger translators, many of whom did not know the composer, are giving new interpretations of works that are being considered for entrance into the hallowed halls of the classical music canon. It is a unique time of re-evaluation.

This brings us to Leonard Bernstein, who was both a composer and a performer, frequently a performer of his own music. The worldwide centennial celebrations in 2018–19 make a reassessment of Bernstein's compositions inevitable. Will all, or any, of his three symphonies become part of the canon in the decades after his centenary? His violin concerto (called *Serenade After Plato's "Symposium"*) received hundreds of performances during the centenary, and now that tens of thousands of people have newly heard it, will this have a long-term effect on future performances, or will the classical music world be satisfied by the Symphonic Dances from *West Side Story* and the Overture to *Candide*? Only time will tell.

Leonard Bernstein the performer and on-camera host brings up the more ephemeral aspect of his career. As someone who worked at his side for eighteen years, I was recently asked to introduce and discuss Bernstein's television appearances when he served as host, teacher, conductor, and (occasionally) composer in his series of Young People's Concerts (1958–1972). I had an immediate response to what I was looking at (in addition to what I was hearing).

The New York Philharmonic in 1958 was an ensemble made up exclusively of white men. Ten years later, in the television series, you can see a single African-American male, in the back of the second-violin section, and a lone woman, in the bass section. The on-camera audience was seemingly one hundred percent Caucasian. On the Christmas Day 1967 telecast, another woman can be seen, in the cello section, and a close-up of the audience showed us an African-American girl. (It should be noted that in 1962, Leopold Stokowski famously created the American Symphony Orchestra, which performed in Carnegie Hall and in which half the musicians were women.)

Earlier I spoke of the unchanging nature of classical music concerts and its central repertory during my lifetime—except for one important thing: racial and gender equality. The New York Philharmonic was, like many orchestras, slow to find diversity among its ranks and its audiences and, because of its large television viewership, projected classical music as white and male—even though women made up a larger percentage of its audience. Bernstein was not solely in charge of hiring new players. That process involved audition committees, and as much as many people wanted diversity, there were traditions that had to be challenged and a question of the applicant pool itself. (Bernstein was famous for championing women and people of color throughout his life.)

As of this writing the New York Philharmonic has forty-four women and fifty men on its fixed roster. The racial mix continues to spread through the world's ensembles. Women soloists have been interpreting the masterpieces composed by men for many decades, and the post of music director is slowly opening to women as well as men, though this is the last bastion of the male-dominated world of classical music performance. In the middle of the twentieth century, black conductors like Dean Dixon, Henry Lewis, and James DePriest broke racial barriers all over the world, much as Seiji Ozawa and Zubin Mehta did. Nonwhite, non-European men could conduct the central repertory composed exclusively by white European men and be lauded for it, just as women are finally being welcomed—sought after, actually—today. We are invited to listen to the music in translation and marvel at the various ways it passes through the minds and hearts of people regardless of gender, age, race, or cultural heritage.

While there is no denying that the central repertory was composed by a subset of the world's population, the fact that it speaks to all people is heartening; that it welcomes those who are not Caucasian is more to the point. Music requires interpretation to stay alive and an audience to hear it and to respond to whoever is presenting it. It is, once again, invisible, and all the talk of "German" music, or "American" music, or, indeed, "men's" music will always be a simplification. Jacques Offenbach was German, not French. Beethoven was German, not Viennese. Ravel's mother was Basque, and John Philip Sousa's father was born in Seville and his mother in Darmstadt.

And while it is absolutely true that the composers of the core repertory are 100 percent male, it's a bit more complicated than that. Wagner's strength and support system for his greatest masterpieces were rooted in his relationship with Cosima, his life partner. She, it should be noted, was the daughter of Franz Liszt and the former wife of one of the greatest performers of her epoch, the aforementioned Hans von Bülow. She did not just sit back and do her needlepoint while Wagner was composing and playing his music on the piano. The same is true of Verdi and Giuseppina Strepponi. She was one of the greatest opera singers of her age who in retirement was a sought-after vocal teacher living in Paris with Verdi for twelve years and then quietly marrying him. A fiercely independent woman, she, too, would have been both an inspiration and a severe and loving critic of every note Verdi composed. She undoubtedly was the very first person to sing his latest sketches or to use her experience to guide certain choices her husband was making in his last masterpieces. The list could go on with Erich Wolfgang Korngold and Luzie, Mahler and Alma, Richard Strauss and Pauline.

This, of course, in no way makes up for the sexism that kept women from entering the all-male compositional world of classical music, but the vast majority of its composers counted on women for steadfast support, inspiration, criticism, and nourishment. The gay Tchaikovsky depended on Nadezhda von Meck's financial and unwavering emotional support over a thirteen-year period. They never met, but exchanged over 1,200 letters between 1877 and 1890, during which time she sent him a monthly stipend. Von Meck died two months after learning that Tchaikovsky had passed away late in 1892. It is doubtful that without her we would have many of the masterpieces we value so highly today. Yet it remains a sad fact of Western musical history that we will never know what so many talented women like Alma Schindler (Mahler) and Clara Wieck (Schumann) might have accomplished for their own sake had they been given the same opportunities afforded to men.

By the twentieth century, life partners were not necessarily women. Benjamin Britten's muse and life partner was the tenor Peter Pears. Gian Carlo Menotti was looked after by Samuel Barber when he first entered the Curtis Institute of Music as a frightened teenager who spoke no English. (Menotti recalled the moment when the slightly older Barber, upon seeing the young man's distress, said in a kind voice, "*Vous êtes Italien?*") After years of open domestic partnership, it was Gian Carlo who came to the rescue of his beloved Sam when, after the universal savaging of Barber's 1966 opera, *Antony and Cleopatra,* Menotti edited and directed a new version in 1977 that cut and rearranged much of the music, years after they had stopped living together. Composing, a solitary and sometimes lonely profession, understandably needs some kind of social interaction and moral support.

Inevitably this will bring us to something we alluded to earlier: the question of the character and personal lives of the composers, and how all of us navigate inconsistent criteria when it comes to music we love, the person who wrote it, and how it was used. We are always translating the translation, after all. Some people think Wagner's villains Mime and Albe-rich are meant to be Jews. I always heard them simply as two-dimensional villains; but I am not Jewish, nor did I live through World War II, when Hitler used Wagner's writings and music dramas to insist on the supremacy of German music and as a justification for murder.

The "Wagner problem" is perhaps the most famous, but we can extend the discussion to every composer you might care about. In general, we would like them all to have been "nice." They were not. Reports of dinner with Mozart make it seem like something we would all find disappointing: he could be quite vulgar and was seldom really paying any attention to the people around him, appearing to be thinking about other things. If you lived in an apartment directly under Beethoven, you surely would have spent a great deal of time complaining to your landlord about noise and the water dripping through the ceiling from his preoccupation with showering. Would that have affected how you heard his music? I have worked with many living composers, and the question "What was he like?" is really difficult to answer—and, ultimately, irrelevant gossip. When Stravinsky wrote that he hadn't really composed his *Rite of Spring* but, rather, was "the vessel through which *The Rite* passed," he was not kidding. Wagner, upon looking at the complete score to his *Tristan,* said much the same thing. "I have no idea how I composed it." Can we (*should* we) separate the art from the artist?

That is another part of the inexplicable nature of music and composition. It does not choose genius based on character ratings or physical requirements of any kind. Deafness would be a condition that would terminate most composers' output. Did it free Beethoven from hearing it acoustically and create the private environment that led him to such unprecedented greatness, or would he have written the same music anyway? Of course, we can never know the answers to these tantalizing questions.

What we do know is that Western classical music has somehow managed to be foundational to the entire world, regardless of national or native cultures, gender, or race. You will find Western symphony orchestras in Istanbul, Tokyo, Hangzhou, and Cairo. And with all the interaction of countries and empires, and the transmission of goods throughout the world, it does not work in the other direction when it comes to music. You would be hard pressed to find Turkish, Japanese, Chinese, and Egyptian ensembles in Vienna, Milan, and New York City. Restaurants? Yes. Music? Rarely. In North Korea, the Symphony Orchestra of the Democratic People's Republic of Korea can be heard playing the symphonies of Gustav Mahler—and, if you believe their website, from memory and occasionally without a conductor.

Where does all of this leave us when we look at the global phenomenon of classical music and its central repertory? Many would call the entire subject immaterial and irrelevant in the face of trillion-dollar entertainment industries. "Who cares?" would be the apt question. Yet the fact is, passion about it for those who *do* care runs particularly high.

The people who view themselves as politically conservative generally do not support using public funds to encourage artists and artistic endeavors, preferring philanthropy and market-driven survival of artists and artistic institutions, if they value the arts at all. And yet, the public might not be faulted for viewing classical music and classical arts as the most conservative expressions on earth while simultaneously seeing supporting the arts as a left-wing, big-government (i.e., liberal) agenda item.

It is, of course, neither. We are dealing with a false dichotomy, which is itself based on another false dichotomy: "conservative" is not the opposite of "liberal," after all. Everyone is conservative and wants to conserve something, and the more passionate you are about conserving that something, the more liberal you are in the pursuit of that belief. If you believe classical music matters, then you might want to be liberal in conserving and maintaining it. Edmund Burke, one of the founding fathers of modern conservatism, wrote in 1790 that we must "reform in order to conserve."

Wherever I travel, the "feel good" segment of the national news—after stories of war, violence, corruption, sports, and weather—will frequently have something to do with the life-changing impact classical music brings to children; or how playing Mozart in a vineyard seemingly makes grapes sweeter and reduces insect attacks; how young people born into poverty are joining a youth orchestra in Venezuela; how military veterans manage post-traumatic stress disorder by playing a violin; or how people suffering from dementia can communicate through music. An entire field of gerontology has emerged in which music is found to be a healing force as old age and various infirmities take hold of the body and mind. Music transcends both and acts as a mysterious pathway backward in a person's life, managing to have a palliative effect that erases corporeality.

And so, classical music remains. It is heard in many ways, of course, but in spite of cutbacks and strikes, and arguments about what constitutes the appropriate music of our time—and consternation at the public's lack of support for much of the music composed after 1930—classical music's central canon is being played live in just about every city and town in the world. Beethoven and Mozart are everywhere to be heard.

We are in a transition, of course—but the world is always in a transition. The difference is we are living in this one. The books have yet to be written that would "explain" our time and give those who have yet to be born the "reasons" for the outcomes. It is a human thing: finding form and structure; seeking explanations; wanting to connect the dots into straight lines, even as we then watch the lines intersect only to create another series of dots. Classical music will always remain because it is an eternal expression of transition and continuity.

In his 2018 book *Heavens on Earth*, the science writer Michael Shermer noted that although we humans are mortal, we are incapable of imagining our mortality. Without that ultimate understanding, we do our best to create explanations, such as religion and philosophy. Humanity's hard-wired stories of magical creatures, struggles against evil, and happy endings—all told through structures and metaphors—go to the heart of music and why it is our ultimate accompanist.

A friend recently told me of her experience sitting in her car, parked in a dangerous neighborhood in Los Angeles with the doors locked and the windows up, waiting for her daughter, who was attending a prep class for college admission tests. She sat there looking at graffiti, bars on windows, and garbage in the street while listening to Beethoven's *Eroica* on KUSC, the local classical music station. There was loss and decay on the outside and Beethoven on the inside. "I heard things I never heard before in the music."

I asked her if she remembered the first time she heard the *Eroica*. "Yes. I was in school in Connecticut and we were taken to Carnegie Hall. It was like my hair was being blown by a gust of wind. I have never forgotten the experience." And so, forty years and many an *Eroica* later, she called a friend, who tuned in simultaneously, and they texted each other about what they were both hearing in two separate environments in Los Angeles. Together they wrote of new impressions of the interpretation they were hearing. She has now added another layer of meaning to the *Eroica*, involving the disparity of life within her city, her relationship with her daughter, while simultaneously reaffirming an unbroken link to young adulthood.

Her story made me think of the first time I heard Beethoven's Symphony no. 3. Amazingly, although I had not thought about it for decades, I told her that it was on an episode of something called *The Bell Telephone Science Series*. Confirmed by finding it on the Internet, "Our Mr. Sun," directed by Frank Capra and broadcast in 1956, used a score that was an amalgam of classical music and atonal "mysterious" music, sometimes using the theremin (or the similar-sounding ondes martenot), the electronic instrument that had become so popular in science fiction films and in the music of the modernist voluptuary Olivier Messiaen.

Beethoven was the principal source of the classical score. Answering the question of "What has puzzled you scientists most about the sun?" came one word, "Energy!"—which immediately cued the opening to the *Eroica*. Energy! I was ten years old. For me, Beethoven's music has expressed cosmic power, even though it was first experienced out of a

tiny speaker in the family television set. The uplifting opening and conclusion of the program came from the finale to
Beethoven's Ninth Symphony, and it, too, I will always asso-
ciate with natural and supernatural forces, discovery, adven-
ture, and triumph.

If you know the *Eroica*, perhaps you remember when you
first heard it. In my friend's case, she was fourteen years old,
the perfect age to be exposed to it, precisely when a young person's physical and mental development can and will perceive
something of its complexity and attractiveness and attach
itself to her life, to travel with her.

If you have never heard it, listen to it now, and ask yourself
what is happening to you. Listen to those opening hammer
throws of E-flat-major chords followed by the rustling strings
that accompany a powerful and yet meandering melody unlike
any ever written before or after it, outlining a chord and then
swerving downward into harmonic oblivion, only to rise up
again. Does that mean anything to you? Is it merely pretty?
If you know that Beethoven had something on his mind that
made him call the symphony "heroic," and that Napoleon
at that time represented to him the rights of humanity and
the overthrow of tyranny, does that in any way change how
you hear it? And when Napoleon crowned himself emperor,
Beethoven was so disgusted that he tore up the dedication, but
he kept the title as an exemplar of *idealized* heroism, marching
inexorably not just to the last movement but all the way to his
last (ninth) symphony. That was when he used words for the
first time in any symphony, words that unambiguously tell us
of our right to pursue happiness: an Ode to Joy—personal,
communal, cosmic, and God-given.

Now, listen to it. What do you hear? Learn who you are by
how you reverberate to a composer who knew he was being

condemned to deafness two hundred years ago and wrote a symphony that summons the hero in each of us. Classical music thus becomes your doppelgänger. It measures your life as it opens up ever-unexpected possibilities, comforting and challenging. "Who are you?" it asks. "Where have you come from, and why do I matter to you?"

Classical music will respond and never judge you for your vulnerability; for the things you are not proud of; for the things and dreams that you thought were lost; for the life you have led so far. Indeed, it will reward your inquisitiveness in asking those questions in the first place, reward your courage in being fully prepared to hear the answers it wisely and compassionately gives you. And when the performance is over, you can choose to return to the music, to say "Play it! Play it again!" and have it bring back memories and add new ones to sit within the old, or you can walk away from the experience and choose to listen to something else.

As we age, we experience and observe both beauty and ugliness, profoundly understanding the fragile nature of life. We see our lives and develop a certain viewpoint: cynicism? nostalgia? understanding? forgiveness? rage?

This is true of the music composers compose and, of equal importance, the way it is interpreted by the musicians performing for you. And then there's you and how you hear it. Ultimately, you are the interpreter of any piece of music, no matter what the intentions of its composer or performers are. This interaction is unpredictable: three dimensions—author, presenter/translator, and responder (you), all proceeding together through time. Music makes no judgments and offers no explanations. That means it's up to you.

At age seventy-one, I conducted Richard Strauss's *Four Last Songs* with the London Philharmonic Orchestra and a young soprano, Angel Blue. These songs were composed when Strauss was eighty-four and was living in Switzerland in the aftermath of World War II. The poems he chose for these songs spoke of sunset, autumn, a lifetime of loving partnership, and ultimate acceptance of the end of life. I had not conducted these songs in twenty years, when the soprano, Kiri Te Kanawa, and I were barely fifty. I first heard them in college, on a recording with Elisabeth Schwarzkopf, and they made a profound impact on me as an extraordinarily beautiful farewell, something equal to the concluding pages of Mahler's *Das Lied von der Erde.* And while Mahler's song of parting emanated from 1910, Strauss was composing his goodbyes in 1948, when I was three years old. This was music of *my* time, and I could (in college) imagine the aged Strauss in his Swiss retreat sitting at the piano while I was banging nonsense on my neighbor's piano in New York, trying to "figure out" the music I was hearing on the radio.

As an eighteen-year-old, I heard the *Four Last Songs* in terms of Wagner and, to some extent, the other works by Strauss that I knew: his trifecta of masterpieces for the stage, *Salome, Elektra,* and *Der Rosenkavalier,* and the tone poems that he composed as a younger man, specifically *Tod und Verklärung* (Death and Transfiguration), which Strauss quotes at the end of the song called "Im Abendrot" (At Sunset). The soprano sings, "Is this perhaps death?" and on the last word, Strauss disinters a melody he composed as a young man some sixty years earlier to describe his imagined postdeath experience.

If we then skip forward to 2017, I found myself restudying the score and looking at my old markings, written in blue and red pencil on yellowing pages. There are technical notes, changes in dynamics required by Strauss's complex tone colors that can easily swamp a soprano, and some notes from

Leonard Bernstein. But what now, at age seventy-one? Is Angel Blue merely the conduit of eternally youthful beauty, because surely she cannot bring a lifetime of experience to each word and turn of phrase? And what of me? Am I pre-nostalgic, imagining what I will feel like should I reach octogenarian status? I already knew about physical decline (not just of myself, but also of my colleagues and contemporaries). Some friends had already experienced death, and others were severely diminished. And Kiri was long retired, and physically could no longer sing these songs, as much as we might wish to hear what she would bring to them spiritually.

There's another matter: Strauss himself. Having heard many recordings of the composer conducting his own works and having watched videos of his last performances (in London around the time of the composition of the *Four Last Songs*), I know he was never a sentimentalist as a performer. No schmaltz from this Strauss. His excerpts from *Der Rosenkavalier*, recorded in the 1920s, would probably be seen as coldly insensitive today. His performances from 1947 with the Philharmonia were exactly the same: play the notes as they come and do not help me.

In spite of my having conducted for more than a half century, in preparing for this performance I was struck by how many choices were before me. I was pretty sure that I was far more sentimental at age fifty than I was at age seventy-one. While I do spend more time lately thinking about life and all its mysteries and apparent miracles, I feel more Strauss-like in presenting these late Romantic expressions as observant rather than participatory. You, the audience, will take care of the latter.

I was put in mind of my experiences with Menotti, whose musical utterances were "conservative" in that his harmonies and melodic gestures were redolent of the nineteenth century. However, it was very clear to me that his inspiration was not Puccini, but was far older—Monteverdi, who was composing in the early 1600s—and that he did not want sentimentality to creep into how we performed his music. He wanted a coolly detached presentation of the emotionality that was evident from the dramatic situations and the centuries of traditions embedded within the melodies and harmonies. Strauss seemed to want this, too. Again: just play the notes.

I was also sure that Angel Blue's appearance, as a young African-American from Los Angeles, would predispose critics and audiences into hearing her in a certain way: beautiful but lacking profundity, something Europeans like to use against Americans. ("Americans know about World War II," Kurt Masur once said, "but we experienced it.")

What I have learned is that how I shaped the coda of each song would determine the effect of each song, the impact of the totality of the work, and the success of the concert itself. As with short songs by Robert Schumann, Strauss gives each song a postlude, a conclusion in which the conductor can set the ultimate balance and commentary after the soprano has stopped singing and there are no more words. Also, I knew the final series of meandering chords that fluttered between various harmonies and E-flat major meant something bigger than "meandering."

That final E-flat is the chord of the hero, the home key of the *Eroica*, and the key of Strauss's "heroic life"—his tone poem, aptly called *Ein Heldenleben*. It was no accident, but an affirmation of a composer's life: self-described as a hero who withstood World War I and, as an old man, had survived the worst event in the history of German culture: World War II. His wife was alive. His son and their Jewish daughter-in-law were alive. Their two Jewish grandchildren were alive. He could die in peace. I did not realize this until I was seventy-one years old, facing this music once again. And it made a difference.

Another thing: these songs came at the end of an orchestral program devised to express spirituality and transformation. The audience would come to the Strauss after hearing Bach's Prelude and Fugue in E-flat Major in a joyous and kaleidoscopic orchestration by Arnold Schoenberg, followed by Hindemith's depiction of the spiritual transformation of St. Francis in his suite from the ballet *Nobilissima Visione*, which, like the Bach-Schoenberg, would be a discovery for the audience (and for the orchestra, too). The second half of the concert began with a symphonic conflation from Wagner's last major work, his Christian Holy Grail opera, *Parsifal*, in a transcription by Leopold Stokowski—familiar music in an unfamiliar garb. All of this would lead the audience to the final transformation, Strauss's *Four Last Songs*, which would also be a comfort, since it was the most famous work on the program.

If I had changed one work, or placed the Strauss within the concert, the impact of the *Four Last Songs* would have been completely different. In other words, we had created a new piece of music for the audience: a four-movement "symphony" by Bach, Hindemith, Wagner, and Strauss. Its arc of historical time began with the opening of the classical music period and ended with a work that, like its composer, survived World War II. This would be the journey, and I would conduct these works with the Strauss as its ultimate goal. The audience's response in going along with us, and accepting our gift to them, was also a gift to Angel, the orchestra, and myself. Appropriately, she received rapturous applause at the conclusion of the concert.

"The church is the people" is a frequently stated phrase among Christians. In that same sense, classical music is the people—refracted, concentrated, liberated from physicality, symbolic, and timeless. It is transactional and always contemporary, making the music itself indestructible.

Ultimately classical music becomes the soundtrack of your life. These will be your stories, a unique compendium echoing as far back as experience itself, and no one else's, even as we might all share in some of them. The composers invented the music and the performers translate it into sound, believing in the various choices necessary to bring the works to life. You, however, are the interpreter. If you do not understand it, accept it, and embrace it, then the music does not exist as a completed action.

Like a status bar when you download information on a computer, if the bar gets to 98 percent and doesn't make it to the end, nothing actually has happened. The electricity in the wire must connect on the other side to function. And you, the listener, are the end of the transference of energy (information) known as music.

It's your decision, after all, to accept or reject its mating call. Each work added to your playlist will become part of your unique story, and the possibilities are unlimited. The 104-year-old pianist Colette Maze said in a 2018 interview for the BBC that the piano had given her everything in life. "The piano is always faithful. It responds. You ask and it gives."

As I write, there is a pervasive worldwide sense of pessimism and rage that is not unprecedented but nonetheless is deeply disturbing. It is likely that in the coming decades many classical institutions must transform their business models or face extinction. Classical music, though, has always depended on kindness and support from people of wealth or from wise governments who believe in it. This is nothing new.

The first two decades of the new millennium have been saturated with books and movies that portray a dystopian future, one that depends on superheroes to save our planet, much as Depression-era comic books and the science-fiction "invasions" of the Cold War era filled popular cinematic and televised dramas. That said, I am convinced that if there is a future in which only two humans are left, one will be singing to the other, who will probably be playing a makeshift drum.

We shall go out with music, because, uniquely, it is who we are.

Acknowledgments

In this book, which attempts to sum up a lifetime of feelings, I can't properly thank and recognize all the people and all the music that has filled my life from my earliest days as a child, before I had any idea of time and place or a sense of self. That music has given me a sense of who I am should be sufficient in acknowledging its power and the comfort it has given me.

This book, however, is more the product of a request from my editor, Jonathan Segal, at Alfred A. Knopf. He is a music lover who simply wants to know more about it. He is curious to know how a musician hears music and how, perhaps, he can benefit from that knowledge. This is the result, even though I know that music is both universal and intensely private. How can I know what he is hearing? Indeed, writing this book has made me ask that question of myself. What am I hearing, and why did classical music call out to me from the moment I first heard it—mostly in snippets of themes heard on television, and then on recordings at home and at the homes of friends of my brother, Bob, three years older and my first inadvertent mentor?

I say "inadvertent" because he probably just liked this music, too; and as someone who studied clarinet in middle school, he belonged to a small group of like-minded people who played and listened to classical music. He took me along with him. When he was a Cub Scout, they made me the troop's mascot. He became a lawyer. His kid brother needed to hear and perform music every day of his life.

Grandpa Mauceri was a musician, and he saw potential in me. Baldassare Mauceri had conducted hotel orchestras and taught just about every instrument to the Italian-American population of Brooklyn, walking from house to house and occasionally stopping by our home for a cup of coffee and a few minutes' rest before heading out again to bring music to children. It was he who gave me my first piano lessons, but he passed away while I was still quite young, leaving behind a few boxes of his music, thirty-two violins, a cello, and a bust of Enrico Caruso that sits on my mantelpiece.

Aunt Jennie, his daughter and my godmother, brought me to Broadway before my tenth birthday. She introduced me to shows that were revived, making use of their original scenery and costumes, at New York's City Center. That's where I experienced *Oklahoma!*, *Carousel*, *Brigadoon*, and *Annie Get Your Gun*. Soon enough I was attending the original Broadway productions of *West Side Story*, *The Music Man*, *The Sound of Music*, *My Fair Lady*, and *Gypsy*.

On the other side of my family, there was Aunt Rose. It was Rose who asked me to go to the opera with her because she was "tired of uncle Jim falling asleep during act 2." Together with her I experienced a golden age of singing and conducting at the Metropolitan Opera House—capped with the saddest night when the old house closed and then linked a few months later to the glittering opening night of the current house at Lincoln Center. Every one of those singers, conductors, designers, and directors filled my adolescence with epic performances of humanity's stories retold with the greatest music ever composed.

Teachers looked after me, encouraging me forward until I found my métier while studying music at Yale. More people helped me along, opening pathways and saying yes to someone who knew what he wanted but was unsure of being worthy. Both high school and college made me who I am and prepared me for "no." To those who said no I also acknowledge the gift you have given me.

Teaching has allowed me to mentor many hundreds of students, and they continue to inspire and challenge me. Music has sat beside me since I was a very little person and continues to be omnipresent as I write these words. Sometimes, when I perform, I climb inside it. Sometimes, when I am in the audience, it climbs inside me. We are good friends, music and I, and as Leonard Bernstein so memorably said, "It never lets you down."

Shortly before he died, Lenny said he thought he would spend the rest of his life teaching. When he passed away three days later, I knew I had a responsibility to carry on some part of what he had done, knowing I could advance only a small part of "the joy of music" he expressed and his belief in the ability of music to make us a better people and make this a better world than it ever could be without our songs and dances.

My young friends David Gursky, Thiago Tiberio, and Michael Gildin, along with Michael Mungiello and my chief cheerleader at InkWell, Michael Carlisle, have read this text, made suggestions, and kept me going to the finish line. My wife of fifty years, Betty, has broken all the rules and read it, too—and approved. That means more than anything else.

Index

NOTE: Page numbers in *italics* refer to illustrations.

Abbado, Claudio, 102
Abbot and Costello Meet Frankenstein, 88
acoustics, 160–1
active listening, 93–4
Adams, John, 167
Adams, John Luther, 87
Agon (Stravinsky), 87, 156–7
Aïda (Verdi), 59, 118
Ailey, Alvin, 23
Alpine Symphony (Strauss), 45
American Federation of Musicians, 145–6
American folk music, 31
American Symphony Orchestra, 181
anagrams, 77–8
ancient music, 14–15
Andante movements, 47–8
Anthony and Cleopatra (Barber), 59, 183–4
Apollo (Stravinsky), 87
Atlas Eclipticalis (Cage), 159
Atmosphères (Ligeti), 125–6
Ax, Emmanuel, 166–7

Bach, Johann Sebastian, 27, 41, 128, 140
  church music, 98–9
  Prelude and Fugue in E-flat Major, 194
  Toccata in C Major, 151
background music, 93–5
Balanchine, George, 23
ballet, 171–2

Barber, Samuel, 59, 183–4
The Barber of Seville (Beaumarchais), *109*, 115–16
The Barber of Seville (Rossini), 115, 172
Barenboim, Daniel, 3–7
Barone, Joshua, 125
Barrett, Lisa Feldman, 93–4
Bartók, Béla, 57, 64, 93
Become Ocean (John Luther Adams), 87
Beecham, Thomas, 44
Beethoven, Ludwig van, 15, 28, 43, 130, 139, 182
  Bernstein's views, 100, 103
  birthday celebrations, 179
  deafness, 57–8, 184–5
  earliest works, 116
  Eroica Symphony (no. 3), 77, 153, 172–3, 187–9, 193
  European anthem, 141
  Fidelio, 58, 101–2, 172–3
  Hoffman's review, 111
  musical notation, 25–6
  Pastoral Symphony (no. 6), 45, 47, 154
  Piano Concerto no. 3, 153
  Piano Sonata no. 23, 172–3
  piano sonatas, 164
  Symphony no. 2, 95, 103
  Symphony no. 5, 53, 60–1, 103, 111–12, 154
  Symphony no. 8, 103

Beethoven, Ludwig van *(continued)*
  Symphony no. 9, 5, 26, 32, 103–4, 160,
    189–90
Bellini, Vincenzo, 43
bells, 37
Ben-Hur, 146
Benjamin, George, 87–8
Berg, Alban, 22, 81–2, 85
Berlioz, Hector, 74–5, 130
Bernstein, Elmer, 146
Bernstein, Leonard, 31, 44, 57, 98, 116, 152,
    180–2
  on Beethoven, 100, 103
  Candide, 161, 180
  centenary celebration, 180
  on conducting a concerto, 170
  on Korngold, 121–2
  Mahler performances, 112
  on musical structure, 76–8
  Serenade After Plato's "Symposium," 180
  Shostakovich performances, 130–3
  television debut, *91*, 100
  West Side Story, 78, 180
  Young People's Concerts, 180–1
Billy the Kid (Copland), 63
birdsong, 41–2
Bizet, Georges, 44–5
Blitzstein, Marc, 97
Blue, Angel, 191–4
blues, 31
body budget, 93–4
Böhm, Theobald, 35–6
Boléro (Ravel), 58, 106, 114
Boulez, Pierre, 29
Brahms, Johannes, 81
  Piano Trio no. 3, 166–7
  Symphony no. 3, 48
  Variations on a Theme by Haydn, 77
brain impairment, 66–7
brass instruments, 36
Britten, Benjamin, 22, 45, 57, 133, 183
Bruckner, Joseph Anton, 4–7, 155–6
Bülow, Hans von, 72–3, 179, 182
Burke, Edmund, 186
Burle Marx, Walter, 121
Bychkov, Semyon, 134

Cage, John, 126
  Atlas Eclipticalis, 159
  4:33, 69, 130
Callas, Maria, 113
Cameron, Sandy, 95
Candid, Peter, *33*
Candide (Bernstein), 161, 180
canonical repertory. *See* Golden Age of
    classical music
Capriccio (Strauss), 118
Captain Underpants, 64
Captain Video, 62–3
Carmina Burana (Orff), 98
Carnegie Hall, 2, 3–7
Castelnuovo-Tedesco, Mario, 121
Catholic Church, 29–30, 98–9
  early music, 15, 24–5
  Jesuit missionaries, 30
Cavalleria rusticana (Mascagni), 53
Cello Concerto (Dvořák), 171
Cello Suites (Bach), 27
centenary celebrations, 179–80
chamber music, 15, 39, 165–8
chimes, 37
choral music, 168
church music, 15, 17, 29–30, 98–9
  Bach's compositions, 98–9
  early music, 15, 24–5
  Moravian music, 30–1
  musical notation, 24–5
  Verdi's Requiem, 99
  See also Catholic Church
Cinderella (Prokofiev), 41
Circus Polka (Stravinsky), 157
classical music. *See* Western classical music
Cleopatra, 59, 146
Clyne, Anne, 129–30
Cocteau, Jean, 84
Coleridge, Samuel Taylor, 15
Cologne Cathedral, 5
comedy films, 88
composers, 182–5, 190–5
  Golden Age canon, 27–9, 43, 139–40,
    182–4
  historical contexts, 114–22, 130–3,
    139–41, 189–90

personal lives and values, 184–5
racial and ethnic diversity, 182–4
Concerto for the Left Hand (Ravel), 58
concertos, 170–1
concerts. *See* live performance
conductors, 179–82
contemporary music, 121–38, 153–4, 187
Copland, Aaron, 31, 57, 63, 182
Corelli, Franco, 113
"Cotton Blossom" (Kern), 77
The Cradle Will Rock (Blitzstein), 97
Cunningham, Merce, 23
Curtain, Phyllis, 176

dance, 23, 171–2
Daphnis et Chloé (Ravel), 39–41
da Ponte, Lorenzo, 116
Das Lied von Erde (Mahler), 191
Das Rheingold (Wagner), 45–6, 82–3,
    86, 94
"Dawn" (Ravel), 40–1
"Dawn" (Schoenberg), 102
Debussy, Claude, 31, 46, 179
    Music for *King Lear*, 155
    Pelléas et Mélisande, 83–5
    Prelude to the Afternoon of a Faun,
        105–6
    solo piano works, 164–5
    Syrinx, 63
    on Wagnerian leitmotif, 83–4
de Mille, Agnes, 23
DePriest, James, 181
Der fliegende Holländer (Wagner), 45,
    62–3
Der Rosenkavalier (Strauss), 61, 118, 191–2
Dialogues and a Diary (Stravinsky), 55–6
Die Mestersinger (Wagner), 43, 46
Dies irae, 118–19
Die Walküre (Wagner), 45, 61–2, 86
diversity, 180–4
Dixon, Dean, 181
Don Giovanni (Mozart), 46, 54, 80, 106,
    173, 176
Donizetti, Gaetano, 170, 173
Don Quixote (Strauss), 75
"Du bist der Lenz" (Wagner), 48

Dunham, Katherine, 23
Dvořák, Antonín, 102, 171

early music, 14–15, 128–9
    Catholic Church, 15, 24–5
    Josquin des Prez, 26
    notational system, 19, 24–5
    period instruments, 15, 24
Ein Heldenleben (Strauss), 75, 193
Einstein, Albert, 49, 52, 101
Elektra (Strauss), 118, 174, 191
Elfman, Danny, 95, 152
emplotment, 60
Eroica Symphony (Beethoven), 77, 153,
    172–3, 187–9, 193
Escoffier, Marcel, 113
Eugene Onegin (Tchaikovsky), 119
European anthem, 141
experimental music, 15
expressionism, 15
extramusical sounds, 170

Fahy, Everett, 154
Falla, Manuel de, 31
Faust (Gounod), 159
Fidelio (Beethoven), 58, 101, 172–3
film scores, 59, 86, 88, 125–6, 146
The Firebird (Stravinsky), 58, 117,
    156–7
flute, 35–6
FM stereo, 145–6
folk music, 31
Ford, Henry, 58
Forsythe, William, 23
4:33 (Cage), 69, 130
Four Last Songs (Strauss), 190–5
The Four Seasons (Vivaldi), 45, 46
Franklin, Benjamin, 58, 170

Gaffurio, Franchino, 9
Garden, Mary, 179
gender diversity, 180–4
Gershwin, George, 31, 45, 116–17, 119
Gibbons, Orlando, 129
Gilbert, Alan, 125
glass armonica, 170

Glinka, Mikhail, 103
Golden Age of classical music, 21–32, 39, 130
  Austro-German composers, 27–8, 43, 139–40
  chronological entry point, 23–4, 27
  chronological exit point, 24, 28, 31
  French composers, 29
  Italian contributions, 29, 140
  white male composers, 182–4
Gone with the Wind, 86
gospel, 31
Götterdämmerung (Wagner), 53, 82–3
Gounod, Charles, 159
Graham, Martha, 23
Greco-Roman civilization, *9*, 12–14, 32, 36–7
  Greek modes, 12–13, 101
  seven liberal arts, 13
Gregorian chant, 25
Grieg, Edvard, 46, 63
Grosvenor, Benjamin, 153
Gurrelieder (Schoenberg), 102, 155, 170

"Hallelujah" Chorus (Handel), 63–4, 99
Hamilton (Miranda), 22
Hamlet (Shakespeare), 54, 135–6
Handel, George Frideric, 27, 98–9
  Messiah, 15, 27, 58, 63–4, 76, 99
  Royal Fireworks Music, 27, 41
  Water Music, 27
Háry János (Kodály), 45
Hawking, Stephen, 52
Haydn, Joseph, 15, 27–8, 46, 53, 77
  Esterházy court, 58–9
  Il distratto Symphony (no. 60), 46–7
  sonata form, 78
  Surprise Symphony (no. 94), 47
Heavens on Earth (Shermer), 187
Herrmann, Bernard, 179
high baroque era, 15
Hindemith, Paul, 28, 57, 94, 117, 194
Hoffman, E. T. A., 111–12
Hoffmansthal, Hugo von, 174
Hold That Ghost, 88
home key, 12–13

Horowitz, Vladimir, 150–1
horror films, 88
Hough, Stephen, 164–5

idée fixe, 74–5
"I Feel Pretty" (Bernstein), 78
Il distratto Symphony (Haydn), 46–7
Il trovatore (Verdi), 173
impressionism, 15, 29
indigenous music, 31
In Search of Lost Time (Proust), 32
instruments, 35–8
  brass instruments, 36
  keyboard instruments, 37
  musical training, *143*, 148–52
  percussion instruments, 36–7
  string instruments, 37–8
  wind instruments, 35–6
Irlbeck, Cayson, 107
Ives, Charles, 126, 133

Janáček, Leoš, 22
Jenkins, Florence Foster, 151–2
Jesuit missionaries, 30
Jeu de cartes (Stravinsky), 156–7
Josquin des Prez, 26
Jurowski, Vladimir, 118–19
juvenilia, 116–17

Karajan, Herbert von, 44
Keller, James M., 125
Kern, Jerome, 77
Kettner, Norbert, 64
keyboard instruments, 37
King David Playing the Harp with Angels Dancing and Playing Music (Candid), *33*
Kirkpatrick, John, 151
Kodály, Zoltán, 45
Korngold, Erich Wolfgang, 28, 57, 86, 121–2, 179, 183
Korngold, Luzie, 183
Kubrick, Stanley, 125–6

La Bohème (Puccini), 84, 172
La clemenza de Tito (Mozart), 96

Lady Macbeth of Mtsensk (Shostakovich), 134
language, 42–3
"Last Spring" (Grieg), 63
La traviata (Verdi), 173
La Valse (Ravel), 58
leitmotif, 80–7
Le nozze di Figaro (Mozart), 80
Leoncavallo, Roggero, 172
Leonore (Beethoven), 58
Les Pêcheurs de Perles (Bizet), 44–5
Lessons in Love and Violence (Benjamin), 87–8
Lewis, Henry, 181
Ligeti, György, 125
Lightman, Alan, 45
listening to music, 93–107, 111–41, 195–6
  audience attention, 94–5, 158–9
  contemporary compositions, 121–38, 153–4, 187
  evolution of response, 130–8, 190–2
  first exposure to a work, 111–30, 138–41, 188–9
  historical context of a work, 114–22, 130–3, 139–41, 189–90
  personal preferences, 128–30, 140–1, 158–9
  preparation, 114, 127–8
  sensory and emotional impact, 16–17, 38–41, 93–4, 96–107, 161–2
  therapeutic function, 66–7, 186–7
  See also live performance
Liszt, Franz, 114
live performance, 39, 94–5, 112–14, *143*, 145–76
  acoustics, 160–61
  audience preparation, 114, 127–8, 158–9
  ballet, 171–2
  chamber music, 165–8
  choral music, 168
  contemporary compositions, 121–38, 153–4
  musicians, *143*, 146–51
  opera, 172–6
  program construction, 153–8, 194

public rehearsals, 140
solo recitals, 163–5
symphony orchestras, 168–71
temporal choices, 159–60
unpredictability, 150–3
  See also listening
Lohengrin (Wagner), 141
Lopez Ochoa, Annabelle, 23
Lorenz, Alfred, 83
Louis XIV, King of France, 29
Louis XVI, King of France, 115
Lucia di Lammermoor (Donizetti), 170, 173
Lulu (Berg), 81–2

Ma, Yo-Yo, 150, 166–7
Madama Butterfly (Puccini), 174–6
Mahler, Alma, 183
Mahler, Gustav, 17, 21, 31, 46, 56, 102, 183, 185
  Bernstein's performances, 112
  Das Lied von Erde, 191
  notational instructions, 25–6, 47
  Resurrection Symphony, 54
  sonata form, 74
  Symphony no. 5, 57–8
  Symphony no. 8, 58, 160
Marie Antoinette, Queen of France, *109*, 115–16
The Marriage of Figaro (Beaumarchais), 115–16
The Marriage of Figaro (Mozart), 115–16
Mascagni, Pietro, 53
Mass in B Minor (Bach), 27
Maze, Colette, 195
McDuffie, Robert, 167
Meck, Nadezhda von, 183
Mehta, Zubin, 44, 181
memory
  historical time, 61–2, 64–7
  musical structure, 77, 78–88
Mendelssohn, Félix, 46, 139, 141, 172
Menotti, Gian Carlo, 183–4, 192–3
Messiah (Handel), 15, 27, 58, 63–4, 76, 99
Metacosmos (Thorvaldsdottir), 124–7, 153
meter, 17

A Midsummer Night's Dream
    (Mendelssohn), 141, 172
minimalism, 15
Miranda, Lin-Manuel, 22
Mitropoulos, Dmitri, 122
modern era, 15, 24, 28–9, 121–37
    contemporary composers, 121–38,
        153–4, 187
    soundscape, 125–8
modern instruments, 15
modes, 12–13, 101
Monteverdi, Claudio, 140, 193
Montgomery, Jessie, 129–30
Moravian music, 30–1
Morris, Mark, 23
Moses, 12
movie scores. *See* film scores
Mozart, Wolfgang Amadeus, 15, 27–8, 88,
    93–5, 169, 184
    birthday celebrations, 179
    Don Giovanni, 46, 54, 80, 106, 173, 176
    earliest works, 116
    Einstein's views, 101
    La clemenza di Tito, 96
    Le nozze de Figaro, 80
    The Marriage of Figaro, 115–16
    Piano Concerto no. 23, 3–4
    piano sonatas, 164
music, 11, 35–48
    exposure, 63–4, 93
    live performance, 39, 94–5, 112–14,
        145–76
    structure, 71–89
    symbol and metaphor, 16–17, 32, 42–8,
        61–3, 67, 87–9
    training of musicians, 143, 148–52
    See also listening to music
musical memes, 86–7
musical notation, 19, 24–6
Music for *King Lear* (Debussey), 155
musicians
    concert formality, 146–7
    group experience, 150–3, 166–8
    partnerships, 177
    training, 143, 148–52
    See also live performance

Music of the Spheres, 12–13
musicology, 26
music theory. *See* structural mechanisms
Mutter, Anne-Sophie, 137

Napoleon, 31, 57–8, 96, 189
narrative, 76
national pride, 43–4
NBC Symphony, 160–1
"Nessun Dorma!" (Puccini), 22
Newman, Alfred, 146
New York Philharmonic, 121, 131, 134,
    153, 180–1
Nilsson, Birgit, 22, 152
Nobilissima Visione (Hindemith), 194
Nono, Luigi, 29
North, Alex, 59, 146
notation, 19, 24–6
The Nutcracker (Tchaikovsky), 58, 63
Nutcracker and the Mouse King (Hoffman),
    111

octave, 13, 17
"Ode to Joy" (Beethoven), 189–90
Offenbach, Jacques, 182
"Ol' Man River" (Kern), 77
Omnibus, 91
opera, 15, 53, 172–6
    happy endings, 101
    potpourri overtures and leitmotif, 80–7
    romantic forms, 102
    theatricality, 175–6
    tragedy, 173–4
    vocal power, 174–5
The Order of Time (Rovelli), 100–1
Orff, Carl, 98
Orpheus (Stravinsky), 87
Ozawa, Seiji, 44, 181

Paisiello, Giovanni, 172
Parsifal (Wagner), 51, 194
Pastoral Symphony (Beethoven), 45, 47,
    154
Pathétique Symphony (Tchaikovsky), 26,
    102
Pavarotti, Luciano, 22

Pears, Peter, 183
Peck, Justin, 23
Pelléas et Mélisande (Debussy), 83–5
Penderecki, Krzysztof, 126
percussion instruments, 36–7
period instruments, 15, 24
Peter Grimes (Britten), 45
Philo of Alexandria, 12
Phyrgian mode, 12
Piano Concerto no. 1 (Tchaikovsky), 72–3, 170
Piano Concerto no. 3 (Beethoven), 153
Piano Concerto no. 3 (Tchaikovsky), 120
Piano Concerto no. 23 (Mozart), 3–4
piano recitals, 163–5
Piano Sonata no. 23 (Beethoven), 172–3
Piano Trio no. 3 (Brahms), 166–7
Poetic Edda, 94
Porgy and Bess (Gershwin), 45
Portsmouth Sinfonia, 152
postmodern era, 15
potpourri overtures, 80–6
Prelude and Fugue in E-flat Major (Bach), 194
Prelude to the Afternoon of a Faun (Debussy), 105–6
Prêtre, Georges, 44
Price, Leontyne, 175
Pridgen, Elizabeth, 167
Prokofiev, Sergei, 31, 57, 102, 117, 136
    Cinderella, 41
    Romeo and Juliet, 172
Proust, Marcel, 32
Prum, Richard O., 41–2
Puccini, Giacomo, 31, 193
    La Bohème, 84, 172
    Madama Butterfly, 174–6
    Tosca, 112–13, 173
    Turandot, 21–2
Pythagoras, 9, 13, 36–7

quadrivium, 13–14

Rachmaninoff, Sergei, 21, 31
    Rhapsody on a Theme of Paganini, 77
    Symphonic Dances, 119

Symphony no. 1, 118–19, 127
    Vocalise, 53
racial diversity, 180–4
radio, 31, 145–6, 160–1
Ratmansky, Alexei, 23
Ravel, Maurice, 31, 130, 182
    Boléro, 58, 106, 114
    Concerto for the Left Hand, 58
    Daphnis et Chloé, 39–41
    La Valse, 58
The Real Life of the Parthenon (Vigderman), 60
recorded music, 31, 39, 145–6
    high-fidelity stereo, 22, 40–1
    long-playing records, 145
Requiem (Verdi), 99
Requiem Canticles (Stravinsky), 117
rescue operas, 101
Resurrection Symphony (Mahler), 54
Rhapsody in Blue (Gershwin), 119
Rhapsody on a Theme of Paganini (Rachmaninoff), 77
rhythm, 17
Rienzi (Wagner), 81
Rigoletto (Verdi), 45, 173
Rimsky-Korsakov, Nikolai, 65–6, 157
Ring Cycle (Wagner), 47, 48, 81–3, 86, 94, 169–70
The Rite of Spring (Stravinsky), 46, 57, 65–6, 117, 131, 184
Road Movies (John Adams), 167
Robbins, Jerome, 23
The Robe, 146
Robin, William, 124
Romantic era, 15
romantic operas, 102
Romeo and Juliet (Prokofiev), 172
Romeo and Juliet (Tchaikovsky), 104–5
Rossini, Gioachino, 45, 115, 172
Rovelli, Carlo, 100–1
Royal Fireworks Music (Handel), 27, 41
Rózsa, Miklós, 43, 146
Rubinstein, Nikolai, 72
Ruslan and Ludmila (Glinka), 103
Russell, Anna, 152
"Russian Dance" (Tchaikovsky), 63

Said, Edward, 7

Salome (Strauss), 118, 191

Salonen, Esa-Pekka, 153, 157

Salter, Hans, 88

scales, 17

Scheherazade (Rimsky-Korsakov), 65–6

Schiele, Egon, 64

Schoenberg, Arnold, 28, 31, 43, 56, 57

   Gurrelieder, 102, 155, 170

   orchestration of Bach, 194

   twelve-tone system, 73–4

Schubert, Franz, 15, 17, 28, 179

   "The Shepherd on the Rock," 152

   Winterreise, 102

Schumann, Clara, *177*, 183

Schumann, Robert, 44, 46, 139, *177*

Schwartzkopf, Elisabeth, 191

Searching for Stars on an Island in Maine
   (Lightman), 45

Second Rhapsody (Gershwin), 119

Serenade After Plato's "Symposium"
   (Bernstein), 180

sexuality, 61–2

Shakespeare, William, 54

"The Shepherd on the Rock" (Schubert),
   152

Shermer, Michael, 187

Shostakovich, Dmitri, 43, 46, 130–7

   Lady Macbeth of Mtsensk, 134

   Symphony no. 5, 130–7

Shostakovich, Maxim, 43

Show Boat (Kern), 77

Sibelius, Jean, 31, 46, 117

   Symphony no. 2, 79–80

   Symphony no. 4, 158

   Symphony no. 5, 158

   The Tempest, 45

Skinner, Frank, 88

The Sleeping Beauty (Tchaikovsky), 41

Smithson, Harriet, 75

solo recitals, 163–5

sonata form, 74, 78–80

Sondheim, Stephen, 78

The Song of Bernadette (Werfel), 57

Song of the Nightingale (Stravinsky), 117

Sophocles, 174

soundscape, 125–8

"Spring" (Vivaldi), 46

Staatskapelle Berlin, 3–7

Star Wars, 86

St. Augustine, 12

Steiner, Max, 86, 122

St. Matthew Passion (Bach), 27

Stockhausen, Karlheinz, 126

Stokowski, Leopold, 146, 181, 194

Strauss, Johann, Jr., 46

Strauss, Pauline, 183

Strauss, Richard, 28, 31, 46, 57, 84, 117–18,
   183

   Alpine Symphony, 45

   Capriccio, 118

   Der Rosenkavalier, 61, 118, 191–2

   Ein Heldenleben, 75, 193

   Elektra, 118, 174, 191

   Four Last Songs, 190–5

   recorded performances, 192

   Salome, 118, 191

   Till Eulenspiegel's Merry Pranks, 75–6

   Tod und Verklärung, 191

   tone poems, 75

Stravinsky, Igor, 31, 102, 117, 130, 156–7

   Agon, 156–7

   Apollo, 87

   Circus Polka, 157

   Dialogues and a Diary, 55–6

   The Firebird, 58, 117, 156–7

   Jeu de cartes, 156–7

   rejection of leitmotif, 83, 87

   Requiem Canticles, 117

   The Rite of Spring, 46, 57, 65–6, 117,
     131, 184

   Song of the Nightingale, 117

   Symphony in C, 55–6

   Symphony in Three Movements, 55–7

Street Scene (Weill), 117, 161

Strepponi, Giuseppina, 182

string instruments, 37–8, 148

string quartets, 27–8

structural mechanisms, 71–89

   Berlioz's *idée fixe*, 74–5

   concertos, 72–3

   film scores, 86

memory and continuity, 77, 80–9
musical memes, 86–7
sonatas, 74, 78–80
Strauss's tone poems, 75
tempo, 76–7, 160
Wagnerian leitmotif, 80–7
"Summer" (Vivaldi), 45
Sunset Blvd., 86
Surprise Symphony (Haydn), 47
"Swanee" (Gershwin), 116
symbolic thought, 42–3
Symphonic Dances (Rachmaninoff), 119
Symphonic Dances from *West Side Story*
(Bernstein), 180
Symphonie fantastique (Berlioz), 74–5
symphonies, 15, 27–8, 53
Symphony in C (Stravinsky), 55–6
Symphony in F-sharp (Korngold),
121–2
Symphony in Three Movements
(Stravinsky), 55–7
Symphony no. 1 (Rachmaninoff), 118–19,
127
Symphony no. 2 (Beethoven), 95, 103
Symphony no. 3 (Brahms), 48
Symphony no. 4 (Ives), 126
Symphony no. 4 (Sibelius), 158
Symphony no. 5 (Beethoven), 53, 60–1,
103, 111–12, 154
Symphony no. 5 (Mahler), 57–8
Symphony no. 5 (Shostakovich), 130–7
Symphony no. 5 (Sibelius), 158
Symphony no. 6 (Tchaikovsky), 26,
102
Symphony no. 8 (Beethoven), 103
Symphony no. 8 (Mahler), 58, 160
Symphony no. 9 (Beethoven), 5, 26, 32,
103–4, 160, 189–90
Symphony no. 9 (Bruckner), 4–7, 155–6
symphony orchestras, 168–71
adaptability, 168–9
conductors, 179–82
extramusical sounds, 170
origins and expansion, 169–70
racial and gender diversity, 180–2
Syrinx (Debussy), 63

Tannhäuser (Wagner), 46, 61
Taylor, Paul, 23
Tchaikovsky, Pyotr Ilyich, 46, 116, 119–21,
179, 183
on Bach, 128
Carnegie Hall, 6
Eugene Onegin, 119
The Nutcracker, 58, 63
Pathétique Symphony (no. 6), 26, 102
Piano Concerto no. 1, 72–3, 170
Piano Concerto no. 3, 120
Romeo and Juliet, 104–5
The Sleeping Beauty, 41
The Tempest, 45
Violin Concerto, 170
Te Kanawa, Kiri, 191
Telemann, Georg Philipp, 94
television, *91*, 100, 145–6, 180–1
The Tempest (Sibelius), 45
The Tempest (Tchaikovsky), 45
tempo, 76–7, 160
The Ten Commandments, 146
Tharp, Twyla, 23
Theorica musicae (Gaffurio), *9*
theory. *See* structural mechanisms
Thorvaldsdottir, Anna, 124–7
The Threepenny Opera (Weill), 117
Till Eulenspiegel's Merry Pranks (Strauss),
75–6
Tilson Thomas, Michael, 158
time, 51–67
emplotment, 60
experiencing music, 51–4
historical time, 54–61
idealized past, 59–60
memory, 61–2, 64–7
Toccata in C Major (Bach), 151
Tod und Verklärung (Strauss), 191
Tosca (Puccini), 112–13, 173
training of musicians, *143*, 148–52
Tristan chord, 115
Tristan und Isolde (Wagner), 62, 155–6,
175–6, 185
trivium, 13–14
Turandot (Puccini), 21–2
2001: A Space Odyssey (Kubrick), 125–6

Un ballo in maschera (Verdi), 76

Variations on a Theme by Haydn
(Brahms), 77
Verdi, Giuseppe, 43, 46, 117, 173–4, 182
   Aïda, 59, 118
   political activism, 97, 174
   Requiem, 99
   Rigoletto, 45
   Un ballo in maschera, 76
   Villa Verdi, 76
Versailles, 109
Vigderman, Patricia, 60
Violin Concerto (Elfman), 95, 152–3
Violin Concerto (Tchaikovsky), 170
visual art, 22–3
Vivaldi, Antonio, 45, 46, 140
Vocalise (Rachmaninoff), 53

Wagner, Cosima, 182
Wagner, Richard, 17, 46, 140, 172–3, 182
   antisemitism, 184
   Bayreuth Festspielhaus, 94
   Das Rheingold, 45–6, 82–3, 86, 94
   Der fliegende Holländer, 45, 62–3
   Die Mestersinger, 43, 46
   Die Walküre, 45, 61–2, 86
   Götterdämmerung, 53, 82–3
   half-sleep state, 94
   leitmotif, 80–7
   Lohengrin, 141
   Parsifal, 51, 194
   Rienzi, 81
   Ring Cycle, 47, 48, 81–3, 86, 94,
      169–70
   symphony orchestra expansion, 169
   Tannhäuser, 46, 61
   Tristan chord, 115
   Tristan und Isolde, 62, 155–6, 175–6, 185
Wagner, Siegfried, 43
Wagner tubas, 169

waltz, 118
Water Music (Handel), 27
Waxman, Franz, 86
Weill, Kurt, 28, 117
Wellesz, Egon, 121
Werfel, Franz, 57
West-Eastern Divan Orchestra, 7
Western classical music, 9, 11–17, 21, 32,
   186–96
   contemporary composers, 121–38,
      153–4, 187
   emotional impact, 16–17, 38–41, 96–107,
      161–2
   Golden Age canon, 21–32, 39, 43, 130,
      139–40
   Greco-Roman origins, 9, 12–14, 32,
      36–7, 101
   metaphoric lexicon, 44–8, 61–3, 67,
      87–9
   modern instruments, 15, 24
   musical memes, 86–7
   national pride, 43–4
   notational system, 19, 24–6
   structural mechanisms, 71–89
   white male composers, 182–4
   worldwide popularity, 30–2, 38–9,
      140–1, 185–7
   See also listening to music
West Side Story (Bernstein), 78, 180
Wheeldon, Christopher, 23
White, Hayden, 60
Williams, John, 86, 127
William Tell Overture (Rossini), 45
wind instruments, 35–6, 148
Winterreise (Schubert), 102
Wolzogen, Hans von, 83
wooden instruments, 36
World War II, 28, 29, 98, 184
Wozzeck (Berg), 81–2

Young People's Concerts, 180–1

John Mauceri, world-renowned conductor, writer, educator, and producer, has appeared with the world's greatest opera companies (the Teatro alla Scala, the Royal Opera at Covent Garden, the Deutsche Oper Berlin, and the Metropolitan Opera, among others) and symphony orchestras (the New York Philharmonic, the Chicago Symphony, the Los Angeles Philharmonic, the Orchestre Nationale de France, the Tokyo Philharmonic, the Israel Philharmonic, the Leipzig Gewandhaus Orchestra, and all the major London orchestras) as well as on the musical stages of Broadway and Hollywood. He served as *direttore stabile* of the Teatro Regio in Turin and music director of the Scottish Opera, the Washington Opera (at the Kennedy Center), the Pittsburgh Opera, and the American Symphony Orchestra in Carnegie Hall. Mr. Mauceri is the founding conductor of the Hollywood Bowl Orchestra, which was created for him in 1991 by the Los Angeles Philharmonic. From 2006 to 2013, he served as chancellor of the University of North Carolina School of the Arts, and for fifteen years he taught at Yale University.

Mr. Mauceri has released over eighty CDs and is the recipient of a Grammy, a Tony, an Olivier, a Drama Desk, and a Billboard Award, three Emmys, two Diapasons d'or, and four Deutsche Schallplattenkritik prizes. In 2000 he was awarded the Berlin Prize from the American Academy in Berlin, and in 2015 he was awarded Columbia University's Ditson Conductor's Award for his five decades of commitment to performing and editing American music. He lives in New York City.